WC,~~

A-Ha's, Awakenings, and
Illuminations on the Path
Of Conscious Living and
ENLIGHTENMENT

Powerful You!
PUBLISHING
Sharing Wisdom ~ Shining Light

WOKE
*A-Ha's, Awakenings, and Illuminations on the Path*
*Of Conscious Living and ENLIGHTENMENT*

# Copyright © 2020

The authors of this book do not dispense medical advice or prescribe the use of any technique as a form of treatment for physical, emotional, or medical problems without the advice of a physician, either directly or indirectly. Nor is this book intended to provide personalized legal, accounting, financial, or investment advice. Readers are encouraged to seek the counsel of competent professionals with regards to such matters. The intent of the authors is to provide general information to individuals who are taking positive steps in their lives for emotional and spiritual well-being. If you use any of the information in this book for yourself, which is your constitutional right, the authors and the publisher assume no responsibility for your actions.

Published by: Powerful You! Inc. USA
powerfulyoupublishing.com

Library of Congress Control Number: 2020900064

Sue Urda and Kathy Fyler –First Edition

ISBN: 978-1-7328128-7-1

First Edition February 2020

Self Help / Women's Studies

Printed in the United States of America

# Dedication

*For those who have awakened,
are awakening, or desire to live
more fully awakened in their lives.
May you find inspiration, peace,
and a clear path through our stories.*

# Table of Contents

# Foreword
## Ruth M. Kent

Have you thought or felt like "I just can't take it anymore" or "It can't get any worse"? "*WOKE: A-ha's, Illuminations, and Awakenings on the Path of Conscious Living and Enlightenment*", is deeply inspiring and joyfully encouraging. Each author brings their unique vulnerability and authenticity, easily touching our hearts and offering a new way forward.

Each story demonstrates the evolution and growth of these amazing individuals when they had the courage to be willing and open to the infinite potential that is within. Whether in a split-moment or over time, they made a choice where they said "yes" to this awareness. It brought about a dramatic breakthrough from once perceived hopelessness and the fear of allowing, to receiving Miracles.

Every day, they choose to use their tools and strengthen the muscle that keeps them grounded and present to the greatness within. They live wholeheartedly not from their ego but from their heart, in love and gratitude.

As you read these stories taken from the authors' real life experiences, you will hear what the ego was believing to be true. The ego will look for the problems because that is its job. Their journey moves us from ego to seeing that we have been given free will, choice. We can ask ourselves "So what is it I choose or desire in this moment". We can choose to go deep within and connect to love and gratitude. It has been written many times that what you focus on grows… expands. It is up to each of us to stop, listen, and take action.

Through 41 years of intensive care/Trauma Nursing and now

in my practice I have seen an intense shift; a desire that is calling each individual I work with to discover their own awakening to their higher or great potential. I have seen this in all ages and both men and women. What is so beautiful about this shift, raising the vibration of each individual and the world as a whole is the presence of compassion and unity, shared with each other. As I read through the stories I noticed each one of these gifted, compassionate individuals released their minds and hearts from the struggle of the past memories and beliefs to align with their purpose and gifts to helping themselves and now blessing others.

As I read through these compelling stories, a message came to me. Stop to ask God, Universe, Source for help and be completely open to listening. Be open to the unconditional love and gratitude. Embrace the power that is present to all, within each of us. Commit to yourself to live life from your heart, in unconditional love.

Have Faith and Believe in your Miracle. Enjoy your personal journey of *"WOKE: A-ha's, Illuminations, and Awakenings on the Path of Conscious Living and Enlightenment"*.

Blessings
In love and gratitude,

Ruth M. Kent

# Introduction
## Sue Urda & Kathy Fyler

Waking up and living consciously is not something that you learn and then forget. Once you step into the realm of a more conscious, more *WOKE* existence, there's no turning back. It's as if a switch has been flipped; the light shines brightly on the path before you, and you know it's only the beginning of the journey. As the title suggests, these authors are *actively* engaged in the art of *living WOKE*, and their purpose is to remain on this soulful path of an aware, enlightened way of being.

Awakenings and A-Ha moments show up in a variety of different ways, and there's nothing typical about it.

For some of the authors in this book, it happened over time, through extreme effort and focused attention. For others, it happened almost immediately due to an unexpected event or a "rude awakening". And for others still, there was a more subtle transformation that seeped in gently over many years and a multitude of experiences.

No matter the form or the time required for them to awaken more fully into their lives, each author took the responsibility as their own—they took it to heart. They nurtured their discovery process and made sometimes painful decisions in order to live with more feeling and truth. They stepped away from judgment and fear that they realized was often self-imposed, and all of them found comfort and peace knowing they were not alone in the quest for the freedom that comes with living a more conscious life.

You are not alone either. As every awakened individual knows, we are all ONE.

Two common threads woven through the stories in this book are courage and faith: courage to look deeply into their own predicament, circumstances, and thought patterns, and faith to know the individual was the only one who held the power to effect change.

*I want to help others through my story* were the words heard most often when we spoke with each of these authors, *I want them to know there's hope*. Choosing to bare their souls was not a selfish act, but one of compassion, empathy, and honor. They each knew their story would serve to inspire, encourage, and assist readers like you. They knew they did not go through the tough and sometimes unbearable happenings only for themselves, but also to be of service in some way—often through the telling of their story and the teaching of the lessons learned.

As students of both yoga and golf, we know it is in the ongoing practice that flexibility increases and the game improves. The more engaged and the more attention given to each movement, pose, and stroke, the more advanced and comfortable the student becomes, and more muscle memory is developed. Soon, the movements are ingrained, the motions are rote, and more enjoyment and freedom are experienced in each moment.

The same is true of *living woke*—the more often we purposefully practice being open and mindful of our intention and attention, the more easily we develop our spiritual muscle memory and the more naturally and freely our lives flow.

Just as we are evolutionary beings, constantly changing, growing, and morphing, so is the state of being woke. It is not a "one and done" occurrence; instead it is an ever-expanding, continuous progression and way of being.

We invite you to open your mind and heart as you take in the words by these courageous and beautifully open individuals. As you read, draw the lines from your own life that will inevitably connect you to the stories. Notice your heart space expanding, your empathy growing, and your own desire to wake more fully into your own unique and conscious way of being. Feel whatever feelings emerge and know that they are here for your highest and best good.

We are humbled by the strength and audacity of these authors and kindred spirits, and grateful that they have found their way together as co-authors in this book, so that you may take part in their journeys.

You are an extraordinary creature capable and deserving of great good. We invite you to step further on your own path of conscious living and enlightenment, now lighted by the words of these authors. And always remember to consciously enjoy the process.

With great love and gratitude for you,

Sue & Kathy
powerfulyoupublishing.com

# WOKE
## is an everyday journey.

# Be Easy with Yourself.

# The Ultimate Love Story
## *Celebrating Life & Honoring Death*
### Crystal Cannon Flores

The most significant lesson my dad ever taught me came three weeks before he died.

I am a child of the 70s, raised by hippie parents who lived life on their own free-spirited terms. The early years of my childhood were spent in Lakeside, an area on the outskirts of San Diego. As far back as I can remember, my parents cultivated what most would consider weird side businesses: temporary tattoos, balloon creatures for parties, feather hair clips—except in our case they were the main source of income. We were poor and my parents were just fine with it. *So badly,* they wanted me to share their love of country living, camping, exploring and brown corduroy pants, but I wasn't into any of it. I wanted to go to church with my grandparents in the city, wear fancy dresses with ruffled socks and patent leather shoes. My grandmother had a mild obsession with Shirley Temple—I loved her for that—and she loved to curl my hair and dress me up. I was her living doll.

When I was ten, my parents decided to go to nursing school in Michigan. We packed a U-Haul and headed for Watervliet, a tiny town of less than fifteen hundred, where my dad's side of the family lives. Such a move would have been an adjustment for anyone, let alone an awkward pre-teen. I wasn't comfortable in my own skin, nor with my new environment. I never did adapt to the Midwest, which was no big deal because five years later we packed up again and moved to Prescott, Arizona. One day after I graduated high school, my parents moved to Las Vegas. Obviously, they didn't have an interest in establishing roots anywhere.

Like many, I had some very turbulent years as a young child which created anger, animosity and harsh judgement towards my parents. I viewed my mother as weak, co-dependent, and immature, and my father as passive and unmotivated. Oftentimes I felt like an outsider in my own family, and I lived for my summer visits with Aunt Patsy. Strong, independent, successful, polished, beautiful, and, most of all, loving, Patsy personified everything I wanted to be in life. As for my parents, they were *more than happy* to ship me off to Louisiana when school got out. And no wonder—I was a judgy, bossy little kid who craved structure and neatly combed hair—they were just trying to enjoy life and how I wore my hair frankly wasn't on their list of priorities.

It wasn't until I became a mother that the judgements began to soften. That's the thing about having your own family—reality hits and you realize how challenging the role of a parent is. Today, you'll hear me describe them as "kindred spirits and true soulmates who never left the honeymoon stage with their own special recipe for marriage."

My parents' anniversary was the most celebrated holiday of the year, with festivities that included a mock wedding cake, the original champagne glasses they toasted with, and the crappy cassette recording of their vow exchange, which my brother and I were forced to listen to. In the later years, they rented nice cars and drove to the Oregon Coast for the occasion, though the cassette player, tape, and glasses were always in tow. In 2011 they took an early retirement and moved to their "sanctuary," Newport, Oregon.

Second only to their anniversary were our birthday celebrations. There was always a *real* birthday cake from a bakery, and a crack-of-dawn serenade from both parents. I lost interest in the birthday song when I became a teenager and wanted to sleep. These days, I wish my phone would ring at some ungodly hour on my birthday.

In August of 2015 I was living a comfortable life in San Francisco, working in corporate sales. My husband and I made a decent income and were enjoying the freedom that comes when the kids are older and independent. Life was busy, distracting, and somewhat unfulfilling.

August 15 is Mom's birthday. I called, we sang, and Mom said she wasn't feeling well. Although she had been sick for several weeks, we weren't alarmed because Mom's health, which had never been the best, had steadily declined over the years. This time her symptoms were nausea, dizziness, and headaches. She had been in and out of the doctor's office and hospital countless times, and they always sent her home, saying she had the flu, a bug, a virus. She should drink fluids and get rest. Finally, on her third trip to the ER, they did a CAT scan to check for an inner ear infection. That evening, my dad called to say they'd discovered a mass on the scan and were rushing her to another hospital that could properly diagnose and treat her. Within hours, they'd found the brain tumor and scheduled emergency surgery the following morning. These are the moments when your life feels like a skit from a movie. I remember exactly where I stood and what I was doing when I received that call.

I also remember speaking to the surgeon after the seven-hour surgery, but I have no idea what she said to me. I vividly recall thanking her profusely, because the way I saw it she had performed a miracle and saved my mother's life. Everything was going to be just fine now, I thought. I also remember the confused look on her face as I smiled and nodded my head like I was listening to her deliver great news. Except the news wasn't great at all.

Shortly thereafter, we all gathered around Mom's hospital bed and waited for the doctor to deliver the prognosis. I figured she was about to present her care plan to get Mom strong enough to go home. Instead, she started saying things like, "primary diffuse large B-cell lymphoma of the central nervous system…a rare, aggressive tumor originating in the brain." Her next words were easier to grasp but much more terrifying. "This type of cancer accounts for only one percent of lymphomas. There's no treatment protocol. She has three months."

I left my job and family in San Francisco and moved in with my parents'. My goal: to teach my dad how to live without my mom. How I would do this, I had no idea. Mom and Dad lived for each other—they breathed the same breath—and shared a love and dedication beyond my comprehension.

I wasn't there to teach my dad anything.

I was there to learn.

On September 25, Dad and I were driving back home from a very long, emotionally draining day of tests and doctor visits. We were too exhausted and heartbroken for words, though I do remember our agreed-upon affirmation that we should all live our lives as if we had a three-month prognosis.

The following morning around eight a.m., my brother Ben and sister in-law Carmen arrived for a visit. Carmen and I were enjoying chocolate chip cookies and catching up while Ben rested from the drive. Then, at ten minutes before noon, my life took a hard left.

I discovered my dad—passed away in his bed.

He wasn't sick.

I wasn't prepared.

Anger fueled my entire body.

I felt like my soul had been crushed.

The rest is blurry.

It was like being stuck in a nightmare, and it was about to get worse. I had to go to the hospital and deliver the news to my mother. It was the darkest day of my life, and I truly cannot imagine what I would have done if Ben and Carmen weren't there.

When I walked into Mom's room, she looked at me and said, "Oh, no, where's your dad? Did he have one of those panic attacks in front of Ben and Carmen?!"

That night, I sat at the foot of my mom's hospital bed, petrified that she might die. I didn't take my eyes off her for the entire night.

Eventually I took Mom home and fully immersed myself in caring for her. I was determined to create an environment that reflected the way my parents lived—unconventionally, free, and fun. I had no idea what I was doing or how to do it but when people visited they would say things like "Wow, I can really feel the love energy in this house."

Eight weeks later, November 20, as I stroked Mom's hair and sang C is for Cookie by Cookie Monster (my favorite childhood song), I knew with my whole heart that we were approaching the end. Before I went to bed I told her she was safe and loved and that it was okay to let go whenever she was ready. At five-thirty a.m. a nudge to my shoulder sent me jumping up and out of bed. Nobody was in the room, nobody had nudged me—but I knew I was being called. I raced up the stairs and for thirty minutes I stroked Mom's face, held her hand and delivered a "keep going" mantra until six a.m. on the dot when she took her final breath.

It was beautiful.

It was heart-shattering.

It changed me on a cellular level.

I felt honored that she'd invited me to walk this sacred journey with her.

My parents will be forever sixty-three.

Theirs is The Ultimate Love Story.

My dad had no interest in learning how to live life without my mom. He stayed loyal to his mission up to the very end. He knew she wouldn't let go and leave him behind so he paved the way for her. Once he left this earth, Mom was free to release from her painful body.

That lesson my dad taught me three weeks before he died…

One afternoon I was coaching him on how to shop for organic produce so he could change his eating habits and take better care of his body. Always so gracious and humble, he listened to everything I had to say before replying, "Your mom and I shop at the local food bank." What?! I started crying and apologizing all over myself—how did I not know this—why didn't you tell me—I can help you buy groceries…I had no idea! He looked at me with the sweetest eyes and said "Crissy, we don't mind shopping at the foodbank, we like it, actually. We get what we need there and that allows us to afford the rent for this house—where we can open our bedroom window and listen to the waves crash. That's what is most important to us."

SIGH…

Since my mother's passing I've made it my life's mission to support and educate families to bring the Human Experience back to the bedside. A hundred years ago we didn't have "death doulas," because we didn't need them. It was just what we did as a community; we supported each other. Dying wasn't a medical event, it was a human experience.

Truth be told, I made a lot of mistakes—I did the best I could but it could have been better. If you've ever cared for a sick parent, you know this to be true—you don't know what you don't know, until you're in it.

I no longer think of death as the opposite of life. I believe death is the opposite of birth. Two significant chapters—both deserve to be honored and celebrated.

I've learned many things since August 2015. In this journey I've learned more about living than I have about dying. I've learned the value of human connection. I've learned how to approach the dying and their families with grace and compassion. Most importantly, I've learned to value the small simple things. Nature is my therapy. Life is my teacher. Love is the glue that holds it all together.

*"Don't be afraid of death; be afraid of an unlived life. You don't have to live forever, you just have to live."* ~ Natalie Babbitt, Tuck Everlasting

**ABOUT THE AUTHOR:** Crystal is a coach, facilitator and death doula dedicated to educating and empowering families to bring the human experience back to the bedside. She is the founder of The Grateful Death™, providing resources, guidance and support for a meaningful end-of-life experience. Crystal is the creator of The Grateful Death Intention©, a downloadable worksheet that allows you to design a personal blueprint for the sensory experience of transitioning, such as the space surrounding you, music, touch, scents, visitors, forgiveness, legacy. It is this stuff we don't generally talk about that Crystal believes is the most meaningful gift you can give loved ones. She resides in Seattle with her husband, two children, and dog Toola.

Crystal Cannon Flores
The Grateful Death™
TheGratefulDeath.Org
Crystal@TheGratefulDeath.Org
linkedin.com/in/crystal-cannon-flores-05a42520

# From Rabbit Holes
# to Reclaiming Power
## Roe Couture DeSaro

Remember Alice in Wonderland, when Alice fell further and further down the rabbit hole? It seemed like she was going nowhere fast, yet, ultimately, she found her wonderland. Looking back at my life, I often feel as though Lewis Carroll wrote that part for me. I *was* Alice, and in my professional life I fell down one rabbit hole after another. Yet those rabbit holes would eventually lead me to my paradise.

It all began in the 1970s, when I was an ambitious young woman with big dreams, visions, and the belief that we could do anything men could do. That belief would propel me to break several glass ceilings on Wall Street, even becoming a VP for one of its top firms.

Breaking into the Boys' Club was invigorating! I felt fearless. I was also young and naive enough to think it would only get better... until the stock market crash of '87 sent me plunging down my first rabbit hole and taught me my first major life lesson.

While many of my older colleagues were scrambling for jobs or even relocating out of New York, I remained determined and positive. (After all, as a married woman in the 80's I didn't have the pressure of being the breadwinner). And indeed, I was soon hired by another company, only to lose my job when it too went under. This happened again and again, with each company merging with or being acquired by an even larger one. Each time, it felt like my "luck" had run out.

I had the same experience when I shifted my search from those big names to local firms where I lived. Moreover, many of these companies were "corporate whores"—the type depicted in the movie *Wall Street*. I couldn't work for a company that I didn't love and respect. Each failure took a bite out of my enthusiasm and beliefs.

Feeling lost, I succumbed to the *NY Times* classified section, desperate to find anything that paid a decent salary. The year prior, I had closed on a three-thousand-square-foot home that my husband and I had custom-designed and built. The pressure was coming up towards my throat and my back was up against the wall. With my security blanket of Corporate America falling apart, I decided to try my hand at being an independent professional, not knowing that this new rabbit hole would suddenly become more like a roller coaster. Instead of sliding down fast, it would become a series of ups and downs, twists and turns. In a nutshell, I learned the hard way that working for yourself is very different from working for a company. I would hit a certain level of income, always shy of six figures, and then—"Bam!"—slam right into a brick wall.

For ten years I struggled to figure out how to do it on my own. When I needed money, I went back to corporate. When the corporate world pissed me off, I returned to entrepreneurship. In the process, I lost my confidence, my courage, my belief system; you name it, I lost it. Each rabbit hole felt wider and deeper than the one before, and I felt stupid to let all the money I'd made in the good times go to waste. I felt I had nothing to show for all my hard work; however, I did have two small children, which raised the stakes even higher.

Then out of the blue, a breakthrough happened. Or, so I thought.

In 1998, I was offered the best of both worlds: a partnership with a stock trading firm. Our company grew to million-dollar revenues and I was ultimately made a partner with E*Trade! Life was grand again, but the rabbit hole wasn't finished with me yet!

On an early September morning under a crystal blue sky, I was sitting in traffic and running late for work. *There has to be a better way,* I thought, which led to, *Why did I return to the corporate world?* Oh yeah, they'd made me an offer I couldn't refuse! As I rushed to catch my ferry to Manhattan, I witnessed the first plane crash into One World Trade Center. Thinking it was an accident, we all proceeded to embark on the boat. For me, it was fear of missing work that propelled me to continue. It was my responsibility as a partner, right?

I never made it to my office. I bumped into my secretary in the lobby, who was crying for her sister who worked at Cantor Fitzgerald on the one hundred and fifth floor. While I was consoling her, a friend grabbed my arm and said, "Run!" It was then I heard and saw the second plane heading straight towards us. I didn't stop until I got to the water's edge. It was a moment of panic and terror I will never forget.

While others fled to get to their boats and escape, I let two go by. I was concerned less with my own safety than being there for others.

But the dock on which we stood was not meant for so many people and began to rock fiercely. People panicked and yelled to the deckhand to close the gates and leave others behind so their boat could dock. I decided to take the next boat, not knowing it would be the LAST one out.

When I finally crossed the Hudson River to the Jersey side, I found a ghost town; the buildings normally bustling with people were now empty.

As I got into my car and turned the radio on, I heard about the Pentagon being attacked. That's the first moment I truly felt frightened. Then the first World Trade Center building collapsed. I watched the second tower fall in my rearview mirror. The highway was a twilight zone. Not a soul was around, only some abandoned cars.

That day would turn out to be a pivotal moment in my life in more ways than one, though I wouldn't realize that until years later. It was the beginning of my quest to rethink my definition of success.

In the years that followed, my once thriving multi-million-dollar stock trading business came to a halt, succumbing to the economic aftereffects of 9/11. This rabbit hole was the worst yet. Totally deflated, I felt like no matter what I achieved, I would lose it, whether by my own fault or outside circumstances beyond my control. For the first time, I thought, *Why bother trying anymore? I will never obtain my life's dreams and visions.*

Once again, I took the path of solo practitioner, thinking that at least I would have more time to balance work and family. In the meantime, I would continue to fall down rabbit holes and hit the brick wall, over and over again.

A few years later, I was given the opportunity to write a chapter for a book called *Empowering Transformations for Women.* The publisher knew about my 9/11 experience and urged me to write about what I had learned from it. I said I would because though my mind was intimidated, my gut was telling me to do it. Many times in the past I had said yes to situations that brought me out of my comfort zone, and each had strengthened me in new ways. This time, it would change my life forever.

As I mentally retraced my steps on 9/11, I started to see the lessons of that day. I saw myself for who I was at the core; I recognized my courage and will to not only survive, but to serve others. It was my innate, God-given ability.

This led to a completely different kind of rabbit hole, one in which I examined other aspects of my life. I realized that whenever I had a meaningful purpose, lived authentically, and didn't second guess myself, I was centered and at the height of my power. I also realized that the only things blocking my success were my negative self-perception, limiting beliefs, self-doubt, and fear. In other words, I was getting in my own way.

This helped me to discover who I really was and what was important to me. I found my true calling, and I gained a feeling of freedom and empowerment like never before. I found my strength once again.

Yet, I still had one final awakening to come.

Up until this point, you see, I had never been completely on my own on as entrepreneur, but an independent contractor. Finding my calling gave me the confidence to go completely "solopreneur," not knowing that it would unearth every single limiting belief I had left.

As a success coach and lifelong personal development geek, I was aware of my mind chatter. I also knew that I alone am responsible for creating my reality. Now it was time for some serious "mirror, mirror on the wall" questions! I began analyzing my thinking, both during my highly successful days and the darker ones.

I knew I was self-sabotaging myself once again, but I couldn't pinpoint the biggest killer of my success until I spent focused, non-judgmental energy on it with a sense of wonder and curiosity.

I felt there was still an old story that had me identifying "who" I believed I was. It was shaping my experiences and forming my expectations as to what I felt I deserved. And, it was affecting my behaviors, choices, and decisions. I knew that my sense of who I was and what is and isn't possible for me was forged by unconscious meaning-making throughout my life. And, though I had dealt with many of them, I recognized that having to self-promote as a solopreneur was bringing up perceptions I hadn't encountered before.

Thus began another quest to find the root of these perceptions, and what I found caused the rabbit holes to start to close *instantaneously.*

I realized I had never given myself credit for any of my accomplishments in life. Instead, the meaning I gave my successes was that I was "getting over" on people. I was a manipulator, a conniver, a street-smart wise girl who was great at selling people, who knew how to win without any intelligence. In short, I was a fake and an imposter.

This is why my life was a roller coaster—I kept self-sabotaging.

I realized that even with all my successes, I suffered from "I'm Not Enough" and "I'm a Failure" syndromes. Moreover, I discovered that I had an emotional wall that had not only protected me from disappointment but also separated me from my dream.

Uncovering these meanings was extremely liberating; it also exposed my gifts. I recognized I was willing to take big risks in life, which increased my chance of having a profound impact on the world. I realized I possess a profound willingness to take on huge commitments which means I also possess a great capacity for success. And, lastly, I realized I am a powerful generative, highly creative visionary, and natural leader who can see great advancement for all of humanity. Suddenly, I no longer felt the fear or held the belief that I was a fake and a failure, not worthy or ready to handle any situation.

Knowing no one can shake my confidence without my permission, and that I am a powerful force of nature, here to have a great impact upon the world for the benefit and blessing of all beings, I was able to reclaim my power.

I found my answer to why I had been successful in corporate and not on my own. I also realized why smart accomplished high-achieving ambitious women fail.

I am not the only one!

As a result of this inner work, my business turned on a dime. The self-sabotaging ended and I immediately took *inspired* action.

Life becomes a whole lot more rewarding when you realize and accept that you alone are responsible for creating your reality.

Today, I am grateful for my ups and downs, for I know I wouldn't have the dream life I have now if it wasn't for all those lessons. And if I'm being totally honest, most of the time it was fun!

Life is a process.

Enjoy the journey.

And, as it says in *Alice In Wonderland*, "Not all who wander are lost."

**ABOUT THE AUTHOR:** Roe is a multi-award-winning entrepreneur, four-time bestselling author, TEDx speaker, influencer, and certified coach. After breaking glass ceilings on Wall Street, she founded Gutsy Gals Get More, a company dedicated to leading service-based women entrepreneurs. Her online and offline community programs are uniquely experiential to help women uplevel their mindset, unleash their brilliance, and create clear marketing messages so they can make a difference while earning wild money and having the time to enjoy it all. As a strong advocate for feminine/masculine balance, Roe has women taking more risks and achieving more than they ever had before, and doing so gracefully.

Roe Couture DeSaro
Gutsy Gals Get More
RoeCoutureDeSaro.com
Roe@RoeCoutureDeSaro.com
Facebook.com/groups/GutsyGalTruthTalk

# I Didn't Wake Up Pretty
## Karen Loffler

I stopped on the landing and burst into tears, my hands still gripping the fold-out mattress I'd been yanking up the stairs. I wasn't crying because the mattress was heavy, but because the sheer action of taking such a giant step, finally, had brought my emotions bubbling to the surface. It had taken me years to pull all the pieces together and admit that I would need to leave my husband of over two decades. The separation had grown over time, bit by bit. We'd both wished for the other to be something or someone else. We'd both hoped that the next day the love we had shared might return, all the while knowing it would not.

I moved into my own little home, a quintessential farmhouse in a mountain town I adored. My new home looked out on scented pines and the distant hills. Soft grass covered the side yard and hosta and lilies surrounded the perimeter, providing a haven for my troubled heart. I questioned whether I was worthy of this lovely place, but my guides told me it would be a place of healing.

I was eighteen years old when my daughter was born. We lived with my mother until she was two, then I found a place for us. We got by. I was in college and she was in kindergarten. I worked; she went to daycare. We found a gentle rhythm. Then I met my husband and became a wife and a stepmother; my daughter became a sibling. We settled into a "raise the kids" routine. The next twenty-three years were filled with struggles, challenges, joys, and triumphs as we enjoyed watching our children grow.

During this time, I became physically strong. We hiked, rode bicycles, padded canoes, and walked the dogs, a lot. The physical strength helped me develop more emotional strength but along came a darkness, seeping in from my past. This darkness manifested in quiet and deep ways, including a PTSD-type depression that wrapped itself around me and would not let go. (In hindsight, this was the beginning of the end of my marriage and the start of my total dismantling that led me to the life I have now.) Finally, after about five years of struggling, my husband literally dragged me to a counselor. My childhood trauma was surfacing, freezing up my body and my emotions. Over the next two years I would try every healing modality, traditional and nontraditional, before I finally found what helped me: Reiki and meditation.

A friend who had also experienced childhood trauma was attending a class based on the book, *Eastern Bodies, Western Minds*. It had changed her perceptions of life, she said, and she'd unraveled her life story with these new understandings. She learned to cry in healing ways. She received Reiki once a week to "shift" the energy. I had no idea what she was talking about, but I knew I needed to get myself better. There were too many mornings when I could hardly see through the darkness to get to the light.

She drove me to the next class. The room held the usual crystals, incense, chanting music, and meditation chairs. I had always been drawn to those things, so it was okay with me. The nervous group talked about energy, perceptions, emotions, and how they affect the body. We shared beyond-this-world events that had happened to us. I spoke of how my deceased grandparents would pull back the edge of the room as easily one would a curtain and peek in to see how I was doing and send me love. I also shared a vision I'd had of my daughter getting into a sledding accident. She was fifteen miles away sledding with friends. In my mind, I saw her get on the sled and slide down the hill; I saw as she was bumped off the sled and landed on the back of her head. I watched her then-boyfriend cradling her and yelling, "Call the ambulance!" I stopped what I was doing and moved to the phone to wait for the call from the hospital.

Twenty minutes later, I answered the call and listened as a scared young man told me there had been an accident and she was going to be fine. I was no longer surprised by such occurrences, as they had happened all my life.

What did surprise me was that this group of strangers I was sitting cross-legged with accepted my story. No judgement, no "You are crazy" or "Better get new meds"—just kindness and a sense of camaraderie. I rarely shared this part of me, so this acceptance felt very comforting. That was my start. I spent the next five years learning about other ways of seeing life. I became a Reiki master, cultivated my mediumship, developed intuitive tarot reading skills, and mastered deep meditation. I learned how to listen to the voices from the other side. A true name eludes me (I sense it as an "All"), through which I was able to receive ideas, words, and images that I know did not originate with me. Some people accepted this gift and others rejected it, but it resonated at the deepest heart of who I am.

During my daily meditation practice a door opened and more voices and images surrounded me. I was now strong enough emotionally to accept them. My guides showed up in full force and ready to chat. The voices (I called them voices but it was more of a knowing thought behind my left ear) were always helpful and friendly and often funny. They provided thought-provoking ideas connecting my traumas and struggles to bigger understandings. The usual message for me was *Your thoughts are in your own hands*. They reminded me I could be happy or sad, frustrated or in a learning process. I could forgive, release, and find my way to understanding that my spirit was never damaged, only my humanness. They guided me to make more conscious choices. I grew to understand my likes and dislikes and my true feelings, and I began to face my skewed perceptions of self. It would be a lifelong journey, and one often marked by struggle.

I questioned how, if at all, one could forgive and release a trauma that happened as a pre-verbal child or five-year old girl. Only sparse snippets of pictures came as memories, yet my adult body remembered. A touch or a scent could close my mind and body down. This, I learned, was called "body memories," and they were powerful, leaving me frozen and curled up in a chair for hours at a time. Learning to unfreeze was the hardest part of my healing. Step by step, I found the courage to unfold a finger, then one arm, a foot. The toughest shift had to happen in the mind. I had to face the tormenting darkness. It took years and a rebuilding of my life and my self. In my new home, I had found the quiet and autonomy to heal.

I read books on meditation, chakras, out of body experiences, and other accounts of women like myself, both healers and divorcees. Growing a new type of awareness, I started having days of calm. I kept feeling as if I was coming home as I drifted off with one of the books or during my daily meditations. I remember one particular meditation where I slipped from my head to my heart. Inside my heart was burning the tiniest of candles, smaller than one you'd see on a birthday cake. My guides told me to kindle my fire; it was too small. I laughed, for indeed the flame on the candle was barely visible. I found ways to kindle my heart's fire. I took simple pleasure in longer bubble baths, gentle self-thoughts, and small steps toward self-kindness. I turned on my favorite songs and danced late into the night in only a tee shirt. I was finding ways to be at peace with my body and life.

During my meditations, I faced the darkness one corner at a time. Feelings and emotions that needed to be addressed came gently forward. I allowed them into my heart. Somedays this would literally shake every muscle in my body; other days there were giant healing tears, the type of release that we all wish would come more often. They were the tears of remembering that we are souls. It was working. My body no longer froze fully, and when I felt the darkness advancing toward me, I could breathe deep and release it.

Everything was going well, until it began to dismantle yet again. After five years, I had begun to believe I'd found myself. Yup, I could see myself in a mirror and say, "Hey, you are doing alright." Along with my new confidence, I had found new friends, a new man, and work I enjoyed. My life settled into a comfortable routine. I was proud of the emotional healing I had accomplished, with no idea that I was on a crash course with a deeper emotional and self-reliant growth phase. One day as I was heading up the stairs, a message from my guides hit me with a visceral bonk on the head. I fell to my knees and heard, *You will move now*. One month later, I was living in a new state.

During those healing five years, several major life events had happened. I left my husband and my divorce become final. I lost my standing in the community. My father committed suicide. I became a grandmother. Losing my job was the last straw and left me all but broke financially. Everything in my life had crumbled in my hands like an overbaked cookie. I chose to listen to the head bonk. I rented my house and moved to another state where I was a fish out of water. This meant losing a man I truly loved because our life journeys turned down different paths, leaving most of my friendships fading in the distance, and starting another new life. Everyone has these life-changing events, and I knew I was not alone. It was simply and clearly time for me to wake up again.

One month was not a long time to pack up a three-bedroom house and make arrangements to move to a new state. It came one fast step at a time, but I was doing okay. I was managing. I meditated and took deep breaths. I was fortunate, I knew, because the Universe wanted this move for me and thus the needed pieces lined up quickly. I had family to help; a job dropped into my lap. I found a little rental where I felt safe. Still, grief and culture shock make for a potent cocktail, and I would spend the first year of my new life working and crying. This grief was deep and wide, from the loss of a childhood to the loss a husband, from the loss of a lover to the loss of a community and place that was so dear to me. The Universe placed me in the most vulnerable state, giving me the opportunity to dig deeper into my heart and mind to cultivate broader healing and understanding.

Knowing this did not make it any easier to fall so deeply into cellular-level emotional pain.

Once again, meditation helped me to release. My practice became more intense and focused on literally shaking out the old dirt and dust and replacing it with warm possibilities. With kindness and self-care, I picked up the pieces once again. I even found it was easier this time.

After a year, I started to get myself back on track. I found meditation and healing groups and musicians and made new friends. I found the courage to be who I am. My new life has brought many new opportunities that I never could have imagined. That first year was not pretty, but I woke up again. Now I wake up most mornings looking forward to new adventures and new self-discoveries. And if the Universe comes knocking, I'll answer the door and offer it a freshly-baked cookie.

**ABOUT THE AUTHOR:** Karen earned her Master's in Creative Studies at Buffalo State College, a degree that encompasses the science of creativity, leadership, critical thinking, and nurturing creative beings. She also holds a B.A. in Creative Writing and an A.S. in Retail Management. From Academic Success Center Coordinator to National Tutoring Association Board Member and from Reiki master to Medium, she has stumbled into fulfilling adventures that develop her skills and gifts. Karen blends her academic education with the exploration of meditation and mindfulness to add depth and insights into everyday life and interactions. She is also a songwriter, poet, singer, wood carver, and a mother.

Karen Loffler, M.S.
Shifting perceptions and unlocking possibilities
Karenloffler.com
karenloffler@gmail.com
Guided Tours for Spirit Journeys: in person or remote

# The Gift
## Linda Feliciano

I fell to my knees on the hallway floor, my body wracked with sobs. It was the most excruciating pain I had ever felt, and through the haze of tears and numbness came the thought, *I don't want to do this anymore. Life is too hard. Why would I come into this life to suffer like this? It makes no sense.* My heart felt so heavy I could swear it was squeezing my lungs right out of my body. I barely had enough strength to breathe, let alone pick myself off the floor. I don't know how long I lay there crying, but at some point the pain and desperation settled into a pool of despair. I just wanted to sleep. For a very, very long time. I remember thinking that I needed help.

Now, when I look back on that time I realize how important that moment—as awful as it felt—was in my journey. Oftentimes something seemingly meaningless or barely noticed in the moment turns out to be a pivotal point. Such is the value of hindsight. I'd had several Dark Nights of the Soul before this, and some since. But this is the one that woke me up to the world beyond my limited 3-D perception. This was the moment that would mark the "before" and "after" in my life.

It was as a result of a painful ending with someone I'd thought would be my life partner. Someone I had an intense connection with and with whom, I found out later, I had experienced many previous lifetimes. A person who, for a long time, I would refer to as "the guy who broke me." Now I refer to him lovingly as "the guy who broke me…open," because he gave me the biggest gift one human being can give to another: the impetus to shift into who I really am.

The Universe had been nudging me for some time—bringing forth difficult circumstances trying to remind me it was time to wake up. Nap time was over. But, what can I say, I do love to sleep!

After those first difficult months, I started looking for ways to feel better. I was so desperate that I was willing to try new things, even things I had mocked in the past, like affirmations and crystals. People came into my life and provided insight. Books came across my path at the very moment I needed them. Some had been in my orbit for some time but escaped my notice until the right time. It was as if, even during my darkest moments, the Universe had been putting everything into place. It was building the house, decorating it, furnishing it, and just waiting for me to move in. First, though, it made sure I got evicted from my old place.

Within a year I found an amazing spiritual teacher and mentor who I am now proud to call my friend as well. I started attending her classes to develop my intuitive skills and started looking at the world in a different way. I started exploring my emotions, something that, as a recovering Catholic, I had been discouraged from doing my entire life.

Indeed, there were many shifts as I continued to learn, grow, and evolve. I started feeling more connected to the world around me, and developed an amazing community of like-minded individuals who consistently love, support, and call each other out on their "stuff."

Don't get me wrong, there were still plenty of days when I genuinely felt that "humans suck!" (I'm a more of dog person.) But I was able to see this as my reaction to something I found disappointing or some judgment I had about the world. It was a reminder that I had more work to do. I learned that enlightenment is not about attaining perfection; it is about the journey; about the process of discovering or, more accurately, remembering the essence of who you really are. And by its very nature, that journey has many detours.

One of those detours, and another landmark in my journey, came in 2015. I had taken an interest in crystals, and I'd even began using them while meditating. Now I wanted to find a way to carry them around without having to put them in my pocket or bag. Though practical and resourceful by nature, I had never considered myself to be creative in the artistic sense; now, I found myself learning how to handcraft jewelry! After I made a few pieces for friends, one of them encouraged me to turn my hobby into a business. At first I dismissed the idea—I had always been happy working for a big corporation and didn't want the responsibility of owning a business. On the other hand, if I had learned anything over the past few years it was that I was capable of doing all sorts of things I'd believed or had been told that I could not do. I decided to give it a shot, and in doing so I learned one of the most important lessons of all.

Though I did sell quite a few pieces, the business never really took off. Yet I still felt amazing because I had looked at it as an experiment from the very beginning. To me it was more about the process of putting myself out there, of doing something different and unexpected. It was about becoming more comfortable with an uncertain outcome.

As I evolved, I started delving deeper and deeper into my emotions. I began to see the connections between my childhood trauma and core wounds and the situations I experienced as an adult. A lot of resistance and fear came up, but by this time I had learned many healing techniques, which I now use to navigate the world in a more conscious way.

During this time I also became interested in Shadow Work. I had always been very conscious of my emotions and felt that no matter how ugly they were, they needed to be felt. It never made sense to me why people demonize "negative" emotions. But, like most people who come from abusive environments or experience trauma, I learned very quickly that my emotions were not only unwelcome, they were unsafe because they provoked a reaction from those around me. As a result, I found myself constantly fighting the battle between being aware of my "negative" emotions and actively suppressing them.

Detachment from others, and more importantly, from myself,

became my strategy for survival. People were always able to connect to me easily. They felt validated by me because I could understand and voice their emotions without judgment. Yet, I never felt connected with them because the basis of most of my relationships was transactional. When people offered or gave something to me, there were always strings attached, or at least that is how I perceived it. Everything, including love, was conditional. I was given love only if I showed obedience, so connecting to people felt unsafe, confining, and disempowering. I didn't have language for it back then, but I knew it didn't feel good. This is why Shadow Work, which is centered on the idea of not trying to bypass emotions, resonated with me so much. It was a way of healing that was in full alignment with who I had always been.

The more I delved into Shadow Work, the more I realized that some of the traits I'd long viewed as flaws were in fact gifts. Shadow Work is not just about uncovering the unconscious core wounds and beliefs, but also the positive aspects of yourself that were repressed or suppressed because they were deemed unacceptable by others or by society in general, or because they mirrored repressed aspects of your caretakers. Whatever the circumstances, you got the message, explicitly or implicitly, that something about you was wrong or unacceptable or unlovable, when it is actually what makes you the unique, powerful, and amazing being you are.

In my case, the aspects in shadow were "Linda the healer" and "Linda the teacher." My first spiritual mentor spent well over a year trying to persuade me to become a facilitator and teacher. I had so much resistance.

I also learned I was an empath and, like most, had always felt responsible for, and burdened by, the world. Empathy is an amazing quality to have, but it requires that you have clear boundaries. I had a lot of the former and none of the latter. Interacting with others, especially when they were in pain, made me feel responsible for their well-being and depleted. I saw suffering in people that others didn't and therefore I felt responsible for fixing it—another wonderful souvenir I picked up during my childhood.

This was something I actively worked on unraveling and, as usual, the Universe stepped in to facilitate. In the summer of 2018, a series of events made my home almost uninhabitable. Cranky, exhausted, and fed up, I decided to get away for a couple of weeks and impulsively signed up for a Shadow Work practitioner workshop in California. It would be one of the most intense experiences of my life, and one of the most fulfilling. I came out of the workshop and—poof!—I was a healer and teacher.

I am not suggesting that this happened overnight. All of the work I had done over the previous years was essential to the shift. However, all the prep work and talk in the world would not have been useful if I had not actively engaged in my life. It wasn't until I jumped into the work during the workshop that I realized it was completely natural to me.

As so often happens in spiritual work, after coming down from the excitement of this experience my first thought was, "now what!?" I asked the Universe for help. I didn't need to know the full plan, but I wanted to understand what the next one or two steps were. And, as usual, the Universe delivered. The Universe is always trying to help and to communicate with us, but we must listen and be receptive to the signs.

This journey is never-ending, and I continue to learn lessons that are at times painful and challenging to navigate. Many of my relationships with friends and family have been tested and a few lost altogether.

The peaks and valleys can be disorienting. Last year I met someone who I believe to be my Twin Flame. And, with the joy and excitement of that came more hurt. Currently, we are in separation, which has exposed some deep core wounds. Yet, in the midst of all this deep work, I stand in the truth that I am living my best life!

The Twin Flame Journey is about so much more than a romantic partnership. It was the help I asked for. It gave me the inspiration and motivation to put my healing work and myself out there. And I now have a level of clarity about who I am and what my deepest desires are that I've never had before. I understand that pain is a part of life, and that when I close off my heart so as not to feel the pain, I also prevent myself from experiencing the joy.

There have been many shifts since that day years ago when the pain of life brought me to my knees. I continue to be amazed at how the Universe always responds when I call upon it. I asked for help and I got it, in many different ways. Some were beautiful, some not so much. I have learned to be more specific about my requests since then.

As I venture through my life, I continue to trust that the Universe has my back and that, even if I get lost, I will always find my way back to myself. It is this trust, this awareness, that I define as being "Woke."

**ABOUT THE AUTHOR:** Linda Feliciano is an evolutionary coach and a trauma and energy healer who is passionate about helping others live more fulfilled and joyful lives. Linda is a Certified Practitioner of Soul Realignment™, ARCH® Energy Healing, and Teal Swan's Completion Process, which she uses to assist her clients discover their soul gifts, heal subconscious patterns that are not serving them, and create lives in alignment with their deepest desires. She teaches the basics of meditation at organizations in the Boston area and serves clients everywhere. Linda provides all of her services in English and Spanish and is committed to making spirituality and self-development more accessible to the Hispanic community.

Linda Feliciano
Luna Healing
lunahealingcrystals.com
lunacrystals@comcast.net

# What's Surfing Got to Do with It?

*Riding the Waves to Wholeness*

Suzanne S. Bailey

When learning to surf, one's goal is not simply to reach the shore, but to maintain equilibrium so they are able to savor riding the waves. Being "Woke" is much the same; it is not so much about getting "there" as it is achieving balance so we can be "stoked" (surfer-speak for euphoric) as we walk through life. As for my own awakening, it was rather like being on a slow boat to China, with many waves, storms, and divine appointments along the way.

I was blessed to be raised by loving parents. Dad was very present and supportive; Mom was loving and kind but suffered from depression, probably a result of her own abusive childhood. While I grew to understand that her struggles were not about me, they did impact my life and my sense of worthiness. I was always striving to be perfect, to have everyone love and approve of me. I followed all the "rules," trying to figure out how best to "do life," yet a part of me always seemed to be asking, Where am I and what am I doing here? I found comfort in moving my body and took up gymnastics and dancing. Being part of a team while challenging my mind and body provided a safe haven through my teenage years, but it also allowed me to hide from aspects of my life I didn't want to deal with, and eventually led to hiding an eating disorder as well.

Some of these issues came out in therapy, which I entered into when my first marriage to an alcoholic ended in divorce. Life got better when I married again and became a mom, the best thing I will ever do with my life. On the outside my life looked normal: husband, two kids, good career, et cetera. But inside I still felt fat, ugly, stupid, and boring, like any good thing that happened was by the sheer grace of God. I had few friends, because who could enjoy my company when I didn't enjoy it? My second marriage eventually fell apart, we lost most of our wealth, and my tank was almost empty.

My challenges also continued to show up in my body, as migraines, depression, and a painful nerve condition I was told was incurable. I was often anxious and unable to be in large crowds. I couldn't even take my daughter to the mall without freaking out from all the noise and people. Then, in my mid-forties, I was diagnosed with a heart condition. Though, it was not life-threatening, the experience made me wake up and pay attention.

Thankfully, I already had a solid spiritual foundation which began with my Christian upbringing. Later, I took workshops and read self-help books, but could never seem to embody what I knew to be true. I was in my twenties when I decided I'd had enough of being the pessimistic, worrywart, perfectionist who never measured up. Why, when I had NOTHING to complain about, did I complain about EVERYTHING? I began studying spirituality with a vengeance. Being a mom accelerated my efforts to change so I wouldn't pass down my negativity to my children.

Things finally clicked for me in a Power of Awareness workshop where I learned that the voices in my head, imprinted on me as a child, were not who I am. I could choose to hear my higher self instead. I learned that "I" choose the thoughts that define me, and those thoughts are reflected in my outside world. I gained strength and clarity; I returned to dance and I found an amazing tribe of friends who not only walked with me through my second divorce but were beacons of lights on my path to Woke as my healers and coaches. I admired their "special powers," but I didn't believe I could ever be like them. That little voice in my head (I call her "Gozelda," my reptilian brain that tries to protect me with fear) was keeping me small.

One day a friend asked me to join her for an energy healing workshop. Though I wanted to go, I was concerned about the cost. When I shared this with my then-boyfriend, he said, "Here is the money and don't even try to give it back." Since I was practicing receiving, I said okay and off I went. Guess what? I learned that not only did I have intuition, I was able to easily read the energy and move it. It felt like I had been doing it my whole life!! I kept studying until Gozelda struck again. *Pay the bills, support your children. How will you ever use this? Everyone else is better, blah, blah, blah.* Then God tapped me on the shoulder in an unexpected way.

While working a corporate event at a lovely resort in Southern California, our team was told to "keep an eye on" one of the directors who had just returned to work after an emotional breakdown. She seemed okay, until one day she wasn't. She was medicated and apparently drinking alcohol as well. Not a good mix. The staff decided to fly her home with an escort that evening, but they had been unable to get her calmed down or sobered up enough to get through TSA. They told me what was going on and, before I knew it, the words, "Let me try to help her," had slipped from my mouth. The Old Suz wouldn't have thought for a second that she could help. *God, use me,* I said as I walked towards her room, *Tell me what to say, show me what to do.*

The woman was a hot mess, crying hysterically about what a bad person she was and how she'd ruined her life. I brought her onto the balcony for some fresh air and deep breaths. This calmed her, but not for long. When the hysteria started again I asked her to visualize the rest of the day—what she needed to do and how good it would feel to be home. For a moment it seemed to be working, then she started to loop again—"I am loser, no one loves me, I don't want to live like this." Feeling like this was way beyond my paygrade, I asked her if I could hold her hand while we breathed together. She said yes. Then I asked if I could put my hand on her forehead. Another yes.

We began again with the visualization of what needed to happen to get her out of the resort. When she fell apart yet again, I asked if I could put my hand on her heart. She agreed and I placed one hand on the front of her heart chakra and the other on her back and began to run energy. I told her that she was loved simply because she existed, and worthy of her heart's desires. That's when she shifted.

"No one has ever told me that", she said, still sobbing but in a new way, "No one has ever touched me like you or cared for me like you have for these past few hours."

The staff was amazed. "How did you do that?!"

Not yet ready to own my path as a healer, I downplayed the experience, saying I'd just helped her relax and focus on what she wanted. Truth be told, I think I was more shocked than anyone else. I finally realized God was telling me, "This is your work, so keep going," and I did. I continued to study, work on my own healing, and slowly grow my faith and confidence.

There were many other profound moments where God stepped in to show me my path. After my second divorce, my home was suddenly and eerily quiet. Once there had been four people living in the large house; now it was just me and "Gozelda" who on my darkest nights whispered to me about all the shoulda, coulda, wouldas in my life. I was determined not to listen to her; instead, I would be brave and do bold things and prove to myself that I could be fun and adventurous. I had worked way too hard and come too far to fall back now.

Years earlier, in Bora Bora, I had seen people paddle boarding and yearned to try it. So one October day, I coerced a few friends to join me for a lesson. From the moment my feet hit the board, I was hooked! The balance it required took me back to my dance and gymnastics days, and I hadn't felt so at home in my body in decades. Forget the "divorce boobs," I decided, I was buying one of these! I got a part-time job to earn my "paddleboard money" and joined a Meetup group, where I met Enrique, a guy with an extra board. When he invited me to go paddling on the lake, my friends freaked out. *It's cold and you don't have a wetsuit. What if you fall in? What if he has bad intentions?* I checked in with my higher self and she said GO! Enrique turned out to be kind and happy to teach me, and I was SO glad I trusted my intuition rather than listening to their voices of fear.

Paddle boarding changed my life! I advanced quickly, though when Enrique first suggested I learn to surf in the ocean, I said, "No way! I am no spring chicken and what about sharks and rough waves?" We continued to train at the lake and then I pulled a big brave: a weeklong vacation to the Outer Banks with ten people I didn't know. I was nervous but I figured if I couldn't surf, I would take pictures and everyone would like me for that, right? I had nothing to lose, and what I gained…priceless. I went out into the ocean, terrified but reminding myself of all I had learned on the lake. When a huge wave came barreling at me, I either had to catch it or get rocked. I caught it! Everyone was hootin' and hollerin', "Look at her go!"

That wave changed everything. It was as if in riding it I had activated my Hawaiian surfer chick from a past life. I had never felt so alive, so invigorated, so *stoked*! I had always felt connected to God when moving my body, but now I had harnessed the energy of the earth in motion to become one with the wave. I was forever changed. Learning to surf at fifty while continuing my path as an intuitive healer and energy coach helped me shift from the girl with the glass-half-empty mentality to the woman with the glass overflowing with joy, love, freedom, and zest for life I never knew was possible.

Today, my health is nearly perfect. All my uncurable illnesses have been reversed and I am stronger mentally, physical, and emotionally than I was in my thirties. In 2016, I had a full cardiac workup and learned the leaky value had healed. When Gozelda show ups, I thank her for sharing and return to my director's chair, where I blend my spirit with my humanity and embody my divine state of riding the waves of life with peace, grace, and gratitude.

Life is really a lot like surfing; no matter how much you learn, every challenge is different and there are always ways to improve and grow. You have to be present, understand your surroundings, and be patient, sometimes for days, as you wait for the perfect conditions. But when you become one with the ocean and are timing it just right, the ride is exhilarating.

As Jesus said, "All these things I do, you can do and more." I am here to help as many people as possible discover this truth and use it to create miraculous experiences and ride the big waves of life with a giant smile.

**ABOUT THE AUTHOR:** Suzanne is a healer with a passion for helping people move out of pain and into power so they can experience peace in their minds, bodies, and spirits. She is a vessel for Source energy, a Reiki Master, and is certified in Healing Beyond Boarders, Awakening Dynamics, and Light Bridge. In 2016, during a shamanic ceremony in Peru, Suzanne committed herself to being "the hands and feet of God." She keeps this promise every day in her practice, combining intuitive healing with energy coaching and belief-sculpting to help put her clients in the driver's seat and create magical, joy-filled lives. She offers individual sessions remotely and in person, as well as group healing programs, workshops, and retreats.

Suzanne S. Bailey
suzannesbailey.com
suzanne@suzannesbailey.com
470-465-0208

# Shedding Old Skin

*Releasing All I was Not
to Become Who I was Meant to Be*

Georgette Damian

A s far back as I can remember, I always had a keen intellectual curiosity. While most kids spent recess playing tag and swinging on the swing set, I could usually be found in the school library with my nose buried in a book. Reading became even more important to me as my parents' marriage began to deteriorate. At just eight years old, I figured out that I could lose myself between the pages and not feel the pain of listening to the arguments behind their bedroom door. The fighting became so frequent that my father finally packed his things and moved out of the house. For a while I saw him every other weekend, then the visits stopped altogether and he disappeared from our lives. I haven't seen him since.

I never realized how much growing up without a father figure had affected my life until I was in my thirties and consciously started analyzing my patterns and my reason for doing things; in other words, why I was the way I was. And I say *was*, because thanks to the healing and growth journey I have undergone I barely recognize that hurt young girl or the driven, hardworking, ambitious (almost cold at times) woman she became.

After graduating high school, I made a "sensible" choice to pursue a bachelor's degree in Economics, a decision that was highly encouraged and praised by my mother. I deeply admired her (and still do) for having raised and provided for myself and my younger sister on her own, and now it was time to step into the life she had been preparing us for. This meant obtaining a degree that would lead to a high-paying job so I could finally remove the financial burden from her shoulders. I graduated with honors in 2008, and any thought that I was not fully aligned with this field of study was dutifully pushed aside.

That same year, the economic crisis hit the job market hard. After a year of searching I landed a job in Mexico City, which meant leaving my hometown and going out on my own for the first time. Though it was exciting to have the space and the time to explore who I was outside my mother's home, my new job was not as I expected. I was underpaid, but it was more than that. I felt that I was not good enough, that my colleagues who had studied in the capital were more prepared than I was. This led me to pursue a certification at one of the most prestigious universities in Mexico City. There, I met a teacher who offered me a job as a financial regulator for the Mexican government.

My feelings of exuberance did not last long, however, for at this new job I often felt I did not know enough and therefore was not worthy of earning more money. This was my pattern, and it would keep repeating itself, no matter how many degrees or diplomas I earned! These patterns of unworthiness were not exclusive to my professional life but permeated my romantic life as well. Up until then, I had never had a romantic relationship. I went out with a couple of men, but after a few dates one of us would inevitably call it off. I also seemed to attract men who were unavailable in some way (i.e. they were about to move to a different city or were already involved with another woman).

Back then, it never occurred to me that these patterns existed, or that they were the result of my father's departure. To me, the problem was Mexico and its patriarchal culture that held women back from fulfilling their dreams. The only solution, I believed, was to leave the country and pursue a master's degree. That, I was sure, would afford me the opportunity to make more money and lead the life I was meant to be living.

In early 2013, I received the acceptance letter to the MBA program at one of the best universities in Canada. I said goodbye to my mom, to my family, and to everything familiar in search of the bright future I was convinced awaited me in the Great White North. Instead, the next two years would be the most tiring and stressful of my life. I resonated with neither the rhythm of the studies nor the demands, but as always I ignored my feelings and pushed through. In 2015, I was thrilled when I received my degree; however, my victory would turn out to be bittersweet, since my internship didn't turn into the full-time job I'd expected. Instead, I spent my days recovering mentally, physically, and spiritually from those excruciating years. I didn't know it back then, but this self-care and soul-searching period planted the seeds of the spiritual awakening I would go through three years later.

When I was offered a dream job as a financial analyst at Cirque du Soleil, I truly believed I had been rescued. At that point I had been unemployed for six months and desperately needed the money; I also wanted to believe that I was finally walking my true path.

The first two and a half years with the company were great, but deep down I knew I was meant to do something even greater. I kept telling myself that in contributing to the creation of these incredible shows I was helping people forget about their problems, even if only for a couple of hours. However, it was hard to connect to that sentiment while chained to a desk and staring at an Excel spreadsheet for eight or more hours each day. I was also under constant pressure to demonstrate improved performance at each quarterly review, even though my salary remained the same. I became resentful, but I was too afraid to move. I didn't believe I would be able to find a job as good as this one, at least not one that would pay me a higher salary. Deep down, I still felt that someone else could do a better job than me. I felt replaceable.

On top of that, I was always tired. The little free time I had was usually spent doing household chores and running errands. I started feeling like I was living my life on a loop; repeating the same day over and over again. I felt like a slave to an invisible, oppressive system that was slowly sucking the life out of me. I didn't realize that I was a prisoner of my own mind; a mind subconsciously run by fear, unworthiness, and limiting beliefs.

My breaking point came in July 2018, one month before my thirty-fifth birthday. I had been working overtime for most of the summer, and it saddened me to be spending those warm sunny days in a cubicle, especially since it's a very short season in Canada. My consolation prize was to go to my favorite restaurants and overindulge in food and wine. It seemed like a harmless vice, until the night I ended up in the hospital with severe pain on the left side of my abdomen. I was told I had diverticulitis, and if my body didn't respond to antibiotics I would need surgery to remove part of my intestine.

This episode shocked me to the core, as apart from those late-night overindulgences I considered myself to be a health-conscious person, following a balanced diet and practicing yoga regularly. Clearly, uncovering the root of my illness required deeper reflection. "Why did I get sick?" I asked myself, "How did I get myself into this situation?" As I went deep down the rabbit hole, I realized I had overeaten in an attempt to squash the unhappiness and dissatisfaction I'd been feeling for some time. The next questions were, "What am I supposed to do now? Throw everything overboard?" I'd worked so hard for all of this, yet here I was, unhealthy and unhappy. This was not what I'd envisioned when I came to Canada, but, like I said, any subconscious patterns that you don't address and heal will follow you to the ends of the earth!

The time for me to face myself had finally come. I acknowledged that there were some deep wounds that needed to be healed before I could realize who I truly was and what I really wanted. As I had in my childhood, I turned to books and other resources for answers. It was in reading about spiritual and metaphysical subjects that I discovered energy healing, including The Emotion Code, which is one of the modalities that I now work with in my energy healing and coaching practice.

My intuition also guided me to do a physical, mental, emotional, and spiritual detox. I did a ten-day Ayurvedic detox that reset my digestive system and cleared my skin. I began a meditation practice that helped reduce my chronic stress and anxiety, and regularly journaled about my feelings and what was really going on inside my heart. It was on these pages that I set an intention to find my life's true purpose. Last but certainly not least, I started working with an Emotion Code practitioner on a regular basis. All of these new habits were truly life-changing.

During our first session he released some of the subconscious patterns that I'd deemed to be part of my personality (i.e. "Type A," competitive, a worrier), as well as trapped emotions that were making me run programs of unworthiness and of low self-esteem. We also released the emotions of sadness, abandonment, and low self-esteem stemming from my parents' divorce and my father's abandonment. After a couple of sessions, I started feeling lighter, calmer, more joyful, and more confident in myself. Moreover, for the first time in my professional life I wasn't anxious about my performance.

It soon became clear that my sacred mission and duty was to share this modality with the world so that they too could experience this incredible joy and lightness. If I had undergone trauma that influenced my every decision, I could only imagine how many others were suffering in silence and without any idea as to why their lives were spiraling downward. I realized how badly I wanted to make a difference in the world, and to do this I would have to leave my corporate job and become an energy healer myself. I'd always had an intuitive knowing that I was supposed to help people and be some sort of guide, though for years this knowing was deeply buried beneath the high expectations my family and I had set for myself. I was now ready to step up and fully own that role.

As I continued to work with the Emotion Code and of a couple of mentors and coaches, everything began to fall into place. I was able to leave the corporate life in less than six months; I came up with the name of my energy healing practice during meditation; and I designed my logo during thirty minutes of free time at work! I even built my own website without any web design experience. In the meantime I continued working toward my Emotion Code certification, which required me to put in a certain number of practice hours. I worked on volunteers and started seeing results right away.

My confidence soared, and I knew I would be able to start walking the entrepreneurial path as an energy healer and life coach. I was no longer dependent on an external source (in this case, my corporate job) for money, since I knew deep within that I could make it happen and be successful on my own as long as I remained in alignment with my soul's mission.

As I conclude my first full year of practice, I often pause to reflect on all the incredible things I have learned. The most important of these is that if we have the courage to look within, ferret out and overcome self-limitations, and listen to our heart's wisdom, the Universe will support us all the way! This is often challenging, but as I stand here on the other side of my inner journey, I can promise you that the rewards are well worth it.

**ABOUT THE AUTHOR:** Georgette's journey into the healing arts began in an unlikely place: her financial analyst's desk at Cirque du Soleil. Despite following the accepted formula for success by getting her master's degree and entering the corporate world, she felt lost and unfulfilled. This longing, and a series of serendipitous events, led her to her current passion as a meditation guide, energy healer, psychic, and spiritual life coach. As a certified Emotion Code practitioner, Georgette helps clients release trapped emotions and connect with their ability to create health, happiness, and abundance. Her holistic approach also includes chakra healing, intuitive tarot readings, and fear reprogramming to assist clients in gaining deeper insights into their internal lives.

Georgette Damian ~ Knowledge from the Heart
knowledgefromtheheart.com
Instagram: @knowledge_from_the_heart
Facebook: Knowledge from the heart
514-834-4973

# Awakening to the Magic of Life
Lisa Stamper

Every day, I wake up feeling so grateful for how blessed I am. Every day, I wake up knowing I am living my best possible life, living out my dream of helping others remember who they are, live from a place of alignment, and return to unconditional love.

In this moment, I am so blessed that I can share my story and my message through this book and hopefully help even more people experience the magic life has to offer.

But my life wasn't always this way.

There was a time when I was disconnected from my truth and completely devoid of hope. From the outside, my life looked great. I had overcome a hard childhood and an even more tumultuous adolescence. I had beaten the odds. But inside I was wasting away, and regularly drinking myself into an oblivion. I truly didn't realize I was self-medicating to numb out the deep pain of my past. I just thought I liked to party.

When I was sixteen, I dropped out of school and moved far from home. I met a man twice my age who also liked to party. He made me feel like a princess and desperately wanted to take care of me.

He took me shopping for new clothes. He supplied the weed I loved using daily.

I fell for it, hard. I thought I'd hit the jackpot. I was loving my life.

Every girl's dream, right?

WRONG.

Looking back, all the red flags were there. A healthy, mature person would have seen them, but I was anything but. I was a kid who, pardon the cliché, was looking for love in all the wrong places. He quickly isolated me from my friends and family. He didn't let me work or go back to school, under the guise of me not needing to do those things because I had him to take care of me. All he asked in return was that I stay home, keep the house clean, look pretty, and have a freshly cooked meal and a drink waiting for him when he came home from work.

I wasn't allowed to make new friends or talk to the opposite sex, because it wasn't "safe". He dictated what I was and wasn't allowed to wear, which was the real reason he took me shopping. One time he asked to look through my old photo albums "so he could see how cute I was," only to have me rip up any pictures that had boys or men in them that were not family members. If I truly loved him, he said, it wasn't right to have other men in my life, even if they were just in pictures. What makes me sick is that I actually did it. All those precious memories gone.

The physical abuse began one night when he didn't like what I made for dinner. In an instant, this man turned from self-avowed protector to complete monster. When the blow landed I was terrified, horrified, and in utter disbelief. Afterward, he apologized profusely and swore up and down it would never, ever happen again.

Only it did, many, many times. And every time it happened I convinced myself it was the last. I convinced myself that it would stop. That he loved me. That it wasn't his fault…I had somehow deserved it.

Finally, 1 could no longer deny there was major problem. With nowhere else to turn and no one to talk to, I called a teen hotline. That conversation made me see that he was clearly an abusive alcoholic and what he was doing to me wasn't okay.

And still, I stayed.

The straw that broke the camel's back came after he spat in my face before pushing me down a flight of stairs. I realized that the abuse was getting worse; it would never stop and he would never change. I knew I had to get away from him before he killed me. The very next morning, I got up as soon as he left for work and threw some of my stuff into a garbage bag. Though I was terrified, I did as the lady from the hotline had told me to do: call a taxi and go to a safe place he doesn't know about. I ended up in a battered women's shelter, which I now know was divine intervention. The ladies there were true angels who helped me figure out how to get my life on track. They found me a safe place to live. They set me up on welfare so I could pay my bills until I got a job. They encouraged me to go back and finish high school, which I did, graduating with awards in Math and Business English! During my final year, I got a job at a spa and fell in love with taking care of people. I had found my life purpose. I went to a private post-secondary trade school to become an aesthetician and from there built a lucrative business. Again, I truly feel all of this was divinely orchestrated.

During this time, I wrote out a list of what I wanted in my life. On the top of that list was someone who would love me wholeheartedly, a true soul mate who was supportive and respected, honored, and cherished me. I wanted all of my relationships to be loving and healthy. I wanted to travel, have financial freedom, and emotional, mental, and physical healing on all levels.

And I seemed to get it.

I met a man and we shared a beautiful house and a family (he had a child from a previous relationship). We travelled often and ate and drank well. By all appearances, I "had it all"—all the things that are supposed to make you happy…except I wasn't. I was taking care of him and his child, literally footing all the bills while he went back to school, which I encouraged because I saw awesome potential in him. I now know that it was a codependent relationship because I was trying to save/fix him while sacrificing myself. Once again, fate stepped in. I went to a client's house who introduced me to angel cards and showed me how to do a reading with them. The reading was completely accurate as to what was going on in my life.

I was totally blown away and knew in my core that it was real. I left her house a changed woman, and excitedly delved into my new passion: spirituality. Suddenly, the many things that I had been "eerily" right about since I was a kid started to make sense. But that's another story for another time.

Through my spiritual studies, I found out I was extremely intuitive, that it was completely normal and that it could help others. The more I learned, the more my desire to numb out left me. I no longer drank. The relationship I was in started to change. I realized that we were great partiers together but not much else. I thought maybe we could salvage what we had if he stopped drinking, but when I brought it up he wouldn't hear of it. That's when I knew we were done.

I was single again and thoroughly enjoying my new sober way of living. And because I was so devastated that my previous partner had chosen alcohol over me, I added "sobriety" to my soul mate requirement. Then, without warning, my world came crashing down. A major health challenge brought me to my knees. After everything I had been through; all the years of unbearable suffering and abuse, this health challenge proved to be just too much for me to handle. I tried to go back to using alcohol to cope, but it only made me feel worse. I was in a dark, dark place. It felt like my life had been stripped, everything taken from me. I found no joy in anything. To get out of bed and face another day was a struggle. It was my rock bottom. I was devastated by what had become of my life. I was not connected to the broadened awareness and intuitive intelligence that I now honor, cherish, and live by.

One night, I decided I had had enough. I went to the kitchen, got a knife, held it to my chest, and dropped to my knees. I called out, pleading for help and begging for death. To think of going on living was too painful. Why had I been introduced to the magical part of life, only to be thrown one hell of a curveball? Even in my desperate state I knew I couldn't kill myself. My family had already endured too much and I refused to be the cause of any more pain. I went to bed feeling defeated and exhausted.

I didn't understand then that I'd entered my dark night of the soul.

A moment of true surrender.

The scariest night of my life.

When I woke, I intuitively knew my call for help had been answered. I was being shown by the divine what to do, literally. I was told to go to a bookstore. When I got there, I was led to buy the *Codependent's Guide to the Twelve Steps*. I cracked the cover. When I read that the process required me to face my past, it felt like my worst nightmare was coming true. How could I exhume everything I had stuffed down, run from, and repressed for all those years? Yet somehow, I found the strength to do it. I started to see what was really going on in my life and why and what I needed to do to change it. I did the work in the book, which was the hardest thing I had ever done, and experienced a deep, profound healing.

I was shown a whole different way of living.

By taking this first step (asking for help/guidance), I had reconnected to my intuition and deepened my connection to the Divine.

And it saved my life.

As I continued to follow this guidance, I was led to my next step, then my next, then my next...until finally, after many years, I've gotten to the beautiful place I am now.

Now I help others lay the groundwork so that they too can move through life gracefully, no matter what shows up.

This means that whatever life has to offer, they have a solid, intuitive foundation from which to navigate and come out the other side stronger, wiser, and more empowered.

After everything I've been through, I got back up again and now my life is rockin'.

I've deeply healed. I've transformed my entire life. I've manifested the life of my dreams, the house I live in, the man I married, and more!

My hope is that this story helps readers know that life is about getting up and how you KEEP getting *the eff* back up, no matter what.

It's about recognizing that we are all incredible beings with unlimited potential to create what we want, but we must listen and follow through on the guidance we are given. I love showing others how all the answers already lie within. I love teaching them how to access these answers by reconnecting to their intuitive intelligence, and how to finally unlock the magic of this life.

Trust me, if I can do it, anyone can.

**ABOUT THE AUTHOR**: Lisa Stamper is an intuitive life coach, spiritual teacher, speaker, and creator of "Your Most Extraordinary Life," a course that helps people heal deeply and remember the truth of who they are and what's available to them. Lisa's passion for her work stems from her own healing journey. After years of self-medicating, Lisa hit rock bottom, an experience she acknowledges as her greatest blessing and the wakeup call she needed to embrace her gifts. She now shows others how they can come out the other side of their trauma and heartbreak healed, whole, and complete. In addition to her other work, Lisa hosts free weekly intuitive talks on her Facebook fan page: Lisa Stamper Mind-Body-Spirit.

Lisa Stamper
Lisa Stamper Mind-Body-Spirit
lisastamper.com
facebook.com/lisastampermindbodyspirit
instagram.com/_lisa_stamper

# The Ultimate Artichoke
## Kim Hoyer

I married at the age of nineteen, a decision stemming both from my Mormon upbringing and dreams of a knight in shining armor. I'd been smitten from the first moment he walked off that plane wearing a crisp navy blue suit and a perfect smile. He was returning from a two-year proselytizing mission for The Church of Jesus Christ of Latter Day Saints, and as was our custom, a group of fellow Mormons had gathered at the airport to welcome him home. I was thrilled to find out that the attraction was mutual. Young and so naïve, I felt like the luckiest girl in the world.

There were a lot of rules in our religion, the biggest being no premarital sex. If you did it, EVERYONE would know. The shame of it would be enough to make you hang your head and never want to show up to a church function again. So within two short months of our meeting we wed in our local temple in Portland, Oregon. I soon found myself caught up in a whirlwind of wedding plans and the infatuation I mistook for love. Any red flags were quickly dismissed, for I was never taught to question anyone's motives or to follow my intuition. And besides, he was so damn alluring.

Our marriage was off to a humble beginning. After a couple of months in the room over his parent's garage, we moved to a small one-bedroom apartment in Springfield, Oregon. I waited tables at a local restaurant to help put my husband through college, without a thought as to whether I would be able to go. Nine months into our marriage I got pregnant with our first child, a perfect baby boy we named Austin Cole. I took a job managing our apartment complex so I could be home with him. I wasn't a fan of the job. I was on call seven days a week, twenty-four hours a day, and since I was onsite I felt like I never left work. While most people my age were going to school, meeting new friends, attending parties, and getting drunk, I was giving notices for nonpayment of rent, citing people for noise violations, and preparing apartments for new tenants.

I did this for four years until my husband got his undergraduate degree and started applying to law schools. By this time I had birthed our second child, Taylor Addison. With two babies just fourteen and a half months apart, some days it seemed like all I did was feed them and change their dirty diapers. Uninterrupted sleep was a faint memory.

Then my husband was accepted to a school in California, which meant moving away from my family and everything I had ever known. By this time we had been married five years and it was anything but a fairytale. We were constantly fighting, and though our battles seemed to be over stupid things, they were indications that we viewed the world differently. While I thought it was okay to agree to disagree, he made it his mission to bring me around to his way of thinking. Sometimes we would stay up until two a.m. arguing until I would finally give in from utter mental and physical exhaustion.

This pattern continued for thirteen years. I thought about divorce all the time, another taboo in our religion except in cases of infidelity or serious domestic violence. My husband was mentally abusive for sure—a master at twisting situations and words to fit his idea of how things should be. There were sporadic instances of physical abuse as well. One night, he threw over the children's dresser in a rage, then threw me down and kicked me in the gut. When our neighbor came over to see what the ruckus was, I was mortified and downplayed the situation. This went on for years, and because it didn't occur every day it seemed manageable. Besides, where would I go? We now had four small children, I had no money of my own, and my husband wasn't making enough to pay adequate child support. I also couldn't help but think, who would want a single mom with four children?

One night, when I didn't react or respond to something the way he wanted, he took the piece of chocolate he was eating and threw it at me so hard it left a welt. He claimed he didn't mean for it to hit me, but it was the final straw. I no longer cared what the consequences were. I was getting out.

At that time I was selling animal bedding to dairy farmers. One day on a routine outing I met one of the farmers and experienced nothing less than a chemical combustion. This man was like a magnet and being around him made my heart skip! This MUST be love, I thought. One night I came home from meeting him to find my husband waiting for me. Unable to pretend anymore, I admitted I was seeing someone. We had always said if we cheated on each other our marriage would be over, and I think this was part of me making sure it really was.

News of our separation, and my new relationship, spread through our small town like wildfire. I could literally FEEL people's disdain for me, including at my church. They judged me for having an affair, but they did not know of the abuse I had endured throughout my marriage. My soon-to-be-ex put on a good show in public, but behind closed doors was a completely different story. He would remarry within a year of our divorce and soon had his new wife hating me as well.

The next four years were extremely difficult. Unable to endure the judgment, I left the Mormon church, which included not only my parents but extended family as well. I church-hopped for a while in an attempt to fill that void, but found that the majority of them badmouthed other churches, even from the pulpit! This unloving attitude left me questioning everything. I began asking people what they believed and why, and I learned that regardless of their denomination or religion most blindly believed whatever their parents had taught them. Disgusted, I decided I was not going to subscribe to what I perceived as judgmental, unloving ways of organized religion. If there was a hell and I was going to it, I was determined to have fun in the meantime!

I moved to Portland, Oregon. The change was a lot to handle, even for a positive person like myself. I was learning a new job and navigating a new city, all while juggling my kids' busy schedules. I was also still dealing with my ex-husband, who since my exit from the Mormon church had decided that I was a terrible person and mother. I would often overhear his conversations with the children and realized he was trying to turn them against me.

In the meantime, I tried my best to help them adjust to our new life. My two oldest, Austin and Taylor, were having a particularly hard time. I gave them pep talks, telling them they would eventually make friends and fit in, and planned fun things for the weekends, but it didn't seem to help. I was also working twice as many hours as I was used to and constantly exhausted. I had a perpetual knot in my stomach and the only thing that seemed to make it go away was the glass of red wine I poured when I got home. Most nights I had two or three glasses, sometimes, the whole bottle. I don't know if I could be called an alcoholic, but I was definitely using it to take the edge off my life.

One weekend, my four children visited their father and only three returned. He had decided to keep Austin, our oldest. I was still reeling from this when my ex-husband sent me an email stating that both Austin and Taylor wanted to live with him. He proposed that he get custody of them, I take the younger two kids, and we zero-out child support. This was completely unfair, as he had a spouse to help with the kids while I would have to pay for childcare. More importantly, I wanted to keep my children together.

I really wasn't worried that he would get custody, even after he served with me papers, as I had been awarded full custody two years earlier. Then the unthinkable happened: Austin and Taylor agreed to live with him. Though I knew they'd been having a hard time adjusting to the move, I was completely devastated.

I had been raised to believe that my sole purpose was that of mother and wife. Now that this was being taken from me I didn't feel like I had a reason to live. I even thought of suicide. However, I was never one for pity parties and I soon got busy trying to figure out my next step. One thing I knew for certain was that I hated my soul-sucking corporate job. I had always been told I had strong hands, and I enjoyed massaging people, so I quit my job and went back to school. And, since I hadn't given up on love, I had found some meditations on YouTube about attracting a partner and listened to one every night.

A few months later I met Landon. He is extremely handsome and had amazing energy; he was also, at twenty-five years of age, fourteen years younger than me. We quickly became inseparable, and I thought life was looking up, especially when my daughter Taylor decided she didn't like living with her father after all and came back to me. I stayed positive and continued with my schooling; I also got a roommate to help with the bills.

The next eight months were among the most fun and exciting of my life. However, although Landon was wise for his age in many ways, he could also be quite naïve and immature. He let the opinions of others get to him and hid the fact that we were a couple. I tried to be patient, but eventually I got tired of feeling invisible and the pressure from his family, who did not approve of the age difference. For all I'd been through, I had never dated anyone who wasn't proud to be with me. Finally I ended the relationship, and though I was the one who broke it off, it was very painful. Now not only had I lost my children, I had lost the first man I loved unconditionally. I was at my lowest of lows.

Why was all of this happening to me? Why was my life turning out so horribly? What had I done to deserve it? Determined to find answers, I turned to YouTube, where I had found such helpful meditations in the past. I started watching videos from Wayne Dyer and Abraham Hicks, but I still felt like I didn't have the answers to *anything*. In my desperation, I cried out for help. Suddenly, there it was: a video pulsing with big bright pink letters and a heart, with the words: Love is the only REAL. This simple truth struck me, cutting through years of pain and trauma and filling me with a peaceful knowing. Truly, Source will use any tool at its disposal to gets its message across! It was a funny way to receive such a profound answer, but it made so much sense. If God is love, and we are all unique emanations that stem from that original source of love, then love is the only REAL. And WE are all love at our core! Everything else is an illusion! All these ideas of separation were just that, ideas… illusions. Suddenly, life became a bright colorful place once again. I was excited to share my newfound message to a sleeping world.

Wake-up! Love is the only real! We are one consciousness experiencing itself in duality, so do unto others as you would have done unto you because they ARE you! My path of awakening was just beginning and I still had much to learn, but at least now I had a foundation. I liken this to being the "ultimate artichoke"; the core of love was always there, I just had to learn to peel back the layers and reveal it.

**ABOUT THE AUTHOR:** Kim is a free-spirited soul who teaches yoga, meditation, tantra, Reiki, and how we can shift our perspective to live happier and more peaceful lives. She understands that achieving our full potential is a transformative journey that requires daily commitment and practice. Kim's business, "Journey Evolve" (JE), reflects this understanding and respects the uniqueness of each person's journey. At JE, Kim and her network of trusted professionals teach clients how to start living more fulfilling lives. Kim's philosophy is simple and effective: change the way we view the world and the world we view changes.

Kim Hoyer
Journey Evolve
journeyevolve.com
journeyevolve@gmail.com
971-506-9889

# My Journey into The Golden Age
### Raasiyanatha David Kenneth Swinson-Coker

S ince the first day I came to this experience I've awoken every morning a little more.

Born in Southern California, I moved up to Mountain Paradise before I could walk.

Played in the woods till the sun went down. Finding adventures all around.

Raised at a biblical church, yawning and nose running, I knew it was not for me.

Twenty years ago I married into Native American sweat lodge family. This opened me to understanding my path, The Red Road.

The Red Road, I understood and felt. It was my path, between Me and Source. For My Honor! For my expansion! For my three daughters! For the greater good of all!

Divorced eight years later, I gave her back to the Creator. Left with nothing, I tossed myself into a pit of despair and had to teach myself to climb out. I remembered the lessons learned, now integrated. Held hope strong.

Free to be Me, Divinely loved and fully supported, I expanded my knowledge, studying the great books of old, bridging ancient philosophy and classical physics. Understanding a little bit more each day, I found it is all bliss, held together by love. I awoke becoming the man I was to be. Raasiyanatha is the name Nandji channeled for me from the Ascended Masters. Raa = Fire; Siya = Passionate One; Natha = To be the Guru.

## My Journey into Love and Bliss

I learned when you feel thirst, fulfill the empty. Replace what's needed, what's been lacking.

Strive to fulfill. Yearn for the wetness of adventure, the wholeness of life. Fill the void, take place of the nothing. Replace boredom with the drink of adventure. Take a sip, one step, move forward, create adventure and make it happen! Grow adventure from a dream. Keep the hope alive. Fulfill the dream. Live the life to live, love life, give. Stand tall, rise above it all.

We are Divine, Sacred, Abundance, Abundant, Love, and Bliss.

## The Time is Now!

A moment just past. Time is flowing ahead. This is now and that now is already gone.

This moment of now is a gift. It flows from the future to the past.

The only true moment is the present. That time is a present, a gift, then gone to the past and on to the next present. Every gift of time is a present. One after another. A new dream. A new memory to remember. A moment to enjoy, to full fill, to make a memory, to make the best of.

## The Season of Fall is Upon us!

The is last Fall of the age; the time when you prepare for winter. The time when the days are shorter. Night lengthens. Cold Winds Blow. The time of remembering winter, the time to come.

Summer bids us goodbye till next year. The season when the last call for a warm mate before winter. When the woman wants a warm and cozy to hold close through the cold nights. Just as the leaves are changing, falling to the ground, so I shed my old habits. I must quench life's thirst each day. Must walk in a good way.

## Create Chance!

We must line up all the possibilities open for chance. Seed in a chance. Gather up what it needs and it will have a better chance of growing into its potentiality. Each spark is a chance for a roaring fire; be ready for it. Be ready for the opportunity of the day. Do what must be done to line up the chance you want to see today. Gotta wake with that morning wind. Don't waste time sleeping in!

The time of the sunrise is a wonderful time. The time of awakening; the time of light.

When we rise with the morning sun, the day goes better. There is more energy and less laziness. Is hard to get up with the first light but totally worth it! Must habit an early productive wake. Must have discipline and practice.

What a magical time to be alive!

Our ancestors prayed for us to be here in this time, as all the prophecies are coming true.

The age is at its end. A time when all the information is at our fingertips; access to wisdom 'round the world in handheld devices. It is a time to learn, a time to evolve past our fog and see the Universe the way it truly is.

An eye-opening age. Will the Creator give us back our Third Eye sight?

Will we be able to change to good? Promote love and compassion for all?

**An Age is at Its End!**

As our solar systems travels on the Milky Way we travel from one spot to another.

As the Milky Way tilts on its axis, our solar system travels up to the upmost.

Then it travels down to its downmost. The shift from up to down is the shift of an age. Moving in one direction, then stopping and moving to another. The end of a time from the man of corn? The start of a time for the woman to return to power and leadership.

**An Age is at Its Beginning!**

A new age will begin, an age of enlightenment, where we can

evolve to use ourselves to our true potential. Using our full brain for that which it was created. Its an opening of conscience, a time of evolution. Unconditional Love and Compassion; True Humanity.

**Awakening!**

The stars align to show us the rise of the burning sun.

Below the Tree of Life, the Seven Sisters point toward the star of the east, the star of David. There, the rise of the burning sun will appear on the dawn of the new age. It will be at its lowest. It will stay there for three days before rising again.

Some say the waters will rise, the earth will shake, the volcanoes will erupt. Much will be destroyed. Some say the sun will burst a solar flare that will do much damage, knocking down satellites and disrupting electricity.

The information age may be at its end, so soak it up, soak it up, soak it up. The wisdom age is upon us so learn, learn, learn.

Will we be ready? Have we prepared?

**A Prophecy Fulfilled**

Seven generations after the slaughter of the people, the mix of settlers and the people return to their native ways. The tribes will unite. The women will return to power. The Third Eye will be opened once again. The corporations destroying the people and the earth will be brought low.

We must unite and stand together against this destruction, for love!

It is like we are in a time illusion. What we think we know is really only what we are aware enough to see. Time in this experience is this experience. This time in the body. The experience of life in this body here on Mother Earth again. This is the time to learn what we need for this experience, to help others learn their experience. I feel that I have been here in time before. I feel I have had experiences on this earth before. I am here to be of service. I am here to share what I have learned. I am here to inspire and help. I am here to help people heal and learn the lessons they need to learn, just as I learn what I came to learn by experiencing this body in this time.

There is so much more to this incarnation. It is about choosing each experience and experiencing it.

Jumping into time's timeline.

Going in for another lesson.

Immersing into the body to experience the ego's lesson. Fulfilling soul contracts.

We are divinely supported. This earth is full of usables. Food and Medicine grow abundantly.

Gifting to receive is much better than taking. Using the Medicine plants in ceremony honors the plant's spirit and opens us up to its magic to help us heal on many levels.

Gathered for good.

Gathered for Love.

Gathered for Healing.

Gathered for Clarity.

Gathered for Wisdom.

Gathered by an open, loving, caring, respectful group of healers, some of whom who did not even know they were healers.

An energy Frolicker, I am.

Releasing Fear.

Accepting Bliss.

Expanding the ever-growing Love.

Love, Compassion, Family.

Bliss, Laughter, Love.

All is in Her Kiss.

Duh!

All that was me is Ridiculous! DUH!!

All I thought I knew is Ridiculous! DUH!

Seventh-dimensional Love. Sipping on her kiss, taking in her love bliss. A vibration so sweet, so all of this. Kiss, taste, lick, nuzzle in her joy, bliss love so sweet. Laugh in the joy. Wherever I go, I know she is everywhere.

The vibration, the pure essence of all Creation, here for us with her kiss of love and bliss. Suckling her kiss, bliss vibration, nurturing, blessing nectar, so good. The embrace is like that of Great-grandmother. Like laying on her lap while she pets your head; safe love, unconditional love, life-lived-freely love.

This is the Love of the Rainbow Goddess I was talking about.
This is the Goddess energy, Shakti!
Aum Sakti Aum Sakti Aum Sakti Aum!

It is whatever you say it is.
It is whatever you think it is.

How you feel creates your environment.
Universal Collective Consciousness.
We are Divine Sacred Abundance Abundant Love and Bliss.

All is Love, Love is All.
All is modes of Love.
Different Reactions Between LOVE and LOVE in different ways and angles of modes.
Now, Here, the Present.
True Now, Reality.
The Gift, Life.
The Chance, the Opportunity to Love.
Be Love, See Love. Love Love Love.
Eyes wide open.
Receiving it all in.
Be here Now.
Fully, with All Senses Experiencing Love, Love, Love, Love.

**Peace and Freedom**

Abundant Abundance, here, now! Be grateful to receive it.
Where my focus goes, my life flows
Sit, stand or frolic in freedom, feeling fully the feelings of Love, Joy, Happiness, Bliss.
Thank Love.

**ABOUT THE AUTHOR:** David is a Reiki Master, Master Electrician, Cherokee Sacred Fire Keeper, and Sacred Medicine Shaman. His birth name, meaning "Be Love," was given him by his first guru, his mom! Raasiyanatha is the name Tapasyogi Nandhiji channeled for him from the Ascended Masters. *Raa* means Fire, *Siya* means Passionate One, and *Natha* means Guru. Being Love is his path; walking heart forward, shining his love light brightly out of his chest. Singing songs of Love and Freedom, kissing the earth with his feet. David's revolutionary view is that: "We are all Multiverselings, a part of and all of the Multiverses! Frolicking through the Divine Healing Energy that is all."

Raasiyanatha David
Journey Evolve
journeyevolve.com/raasiyanatha
youtube.com/channel/UC-9r3PU0fJyp4DUdm66offw
raasiyanatha@gmail.com

# Choose to Lose
## Jodie Schock Penn

We all make choices each and every day. Some are good, some are bad, and some can even be life changing! After years of sleepwalking through life, the day came when I finally woke up and took charge of the choices I was making. I was extremely overweight and didn't really think about the food I ate. It had become more about convenience than making sensible choices.

My dad had been dealing with major health challenges for about nine years and had passed away the July before. The last year of his life was spent in and out of hospitals and it became a string of countless takeout meals and grab-and-go type of dinners for my husband and myself. I had no desire or energy to cook by the time I got home most nights. Anxiety was something new to me, brought on by worry and stress knowing that we could lose my dad at any time. Being an emotional eater, I often turn to sweets to comfort myself.

Early on during that year, I found out that I had high blood pressure, so I was put on blood pressure medicine. At first, it didn't work, so they switched it a few times until we found something that agreed with my body. I wasn't happy about having to take meds, but I also wasn't willing to do anything to change. My mindless choices blended with my lack of exercise, caused my weight to balloon up to 285 pounds. There came a point when everything seemed like a challenge, even the simplest tasks where hard and uncomfortable to complete because of my size. It's funny how you don't really see your own weight gain or weight loss, but you can definitely feel it in the way clothing fits and in your energy level. I was bursting out of size 20 pants and 3XL tops. Maybe I was in denial, but I avoided mirrors and being photographed. When you're not happy with the way you feel, it's hard to really look at yourself. It's safe to say that my doctor was concerned about my overall health. The loss of my dad didn't make me change, and I had no will to change at that point. I had no energy and I was mentally and emotionally drained. I just continued living like a zombie and got though each day the best I could.

The April after my dad passed away, we had another loss. This time it was a family friend who I had always thought of as "healthy". She wasn't overweight at all, her energy level was always great and from my perspective, she seemed to be the picture of health! It was a shock to find out that she just didn't wake up one day. I came to find out that she had been diagnosed with high blood pressure a few weeks before. At 53 years old, she had a massive heart attack and it ended her life. I was 42 at the time, on blood pressure medicine, and not doing anything to help myself. This loss hit my soul in a way that nothing else ever has. I think it's because she was young and healthy (in my eyes) and not dealing with health issues like my dad had been. I truly believe that her death saved my life. It was in that moment that I changed and started putting my health above everything else. I still had a lot of living to do and it was time to get my life back on track! I didn't want to be the next one that my family had to mourn.

**Reducing the Pressure**

Over the years I had tried my fair share of diets and weight loss schemes, but I always ended up sabotaging myself in one way or another. My sister had found a program at her Chiropractor's office that worked for her and she invited me to talk to her coaches. With the support of my husband and my doctor, I went to the intro meeting one night to hear about the program. I learned about their philosophy on food and eating which included a few eye openers! The biggest eye opener was that ALL vegetables are carbs. Why did I never realize that?? Yes, I knew that potatoes, carrots, and all the sweet veggies had carbs in them, but I found it mind blowing to suddenly realize that every single vegetable is a carb! Don't get me wrong, most vegetables are good for you; just not all of them when you are trying to lose weight.

Basically, this program is about balancing protein, fat, and carbs. I really liked the coaches and what they had to say, so I started on the program soon after that first meeting. It was laid out in a way that was easy to follow and there was no guessing. All I had to do was follow their instructions. I lost nine pounds the first week and continued to lose each week! This was the first time I stuck with a program and followed it through. I found the determination deep down and focused on me for a change. My coaches supported me and taught me about food and how to eat. The plan they teach was exactly what I needed to get my health on track, plus it helped me get back into cooking. It gave me the tools I needed to succeed and reach my goals.

My main goal wasn't to lose weight, it was to get my blood pressure under control. Weight loss was my secondary goal. I turned to walking as a way to get some exercise and deal with my emotional eating. I work from home, so snacking had always been one of my biggest hurdles. If a stressful situation came up, I'd distract myself by going for a walk. It gave me time to clear my head as well as remove the temptation of food. With every 15 to 20 pounds I lost, my blood pressure medicine needed to be lowered, so my doctor kept a very close eye on me. Each day I had to email her my blood pressure reading so she could track my progress. She had been my dad's doctor and knew where my health was most likely headed had I stayed on the path I was on. For years, she had been trying to get me to do something about my weight and when I walked into her office for the first time after I started the program, she cried out with such joy and happiness for me! "I could tell from your reading that you lost weight!" She was so excited and kept telling me how proud my father would be!

After nine months on the program, I was down 100 pounds and I was off all blood pressure medicine. My blood work was amazing, and my doctor was so happy that she asked the nurse to take a picture of us together!

After I reached my goals, I quickly phased off the program and went away to visit my best friend and her 8-year-old daughter for a week. That was a major learning experience about how easily weight can creep back on. I let myself enjoy my time away and I consciously allowed myself to indulge in birthday cake and carb heavy foods that I hadn't had since I began my journey. A week at the beach to celebrate an 8-year-old's birthday was a fun way to reward myself. I walked for hours on the beach and even roller-skated for the first time since I was a teenager! I would have never attempted that 100 pounds heavier.

Yes, I indulged, but I wasn't feeding my emotions and I savored every bite. I used to eat and not even taste the food. Food was always more about feeding my feelings than nourishing my body. I love sweets and that is something that will always be with me. The difference now is that I fully enjoy the treats I occasionally eat. I think about the food I eat and make conscious decisions instead of just eating to eat.

By the time I headed home, I knew that I gained weight, because my size 8 capris were feeling a little tight. At my weigh-in two days later, I found out that I gained seven pounds while I was on vacation! It was my first lesson on how *not* to maintain your weight. After that, I went back on the program for a week and then slowly phased off again, this time over a two-month period. I've been on maintenance for eight months now and am doing really well. I keep my weight between 180 and 190 pounds. If it gets close to 190, I really pay attention and cut back on any extra treats for a while. I'm learning that it's okay to indulge once or twice a week, just not every day, because that's when the weight magically reappears!

**Balance and Miracles**

To help me stay balanced in many different areas of my life, I've added CBD to my supplements. After educating myself further, I came to realize that not all CBD is equal. The only way I was going to be able to have a CBD product that I could trust and believe in, was to create my own product that I had full control over. My mom and I own a toxin-free products company, AlphaZelle LLC, and we felt that CBD would be a perfect addition to our offerings. We named this product line, 'Nature's Golden Miracle' because it comes from nature, it's golden in color and we consider it's many benefits a miracle!

Our CBD is created from a unique propriety strain of medicinal hemp that is naturally high in cannabinoids. Nature's Golden Miracle CBD is formulated with THC-FREE Phytocannbinoid Hemp Oil (PCR) which is naturally rich in Cannabidiol (CBD), and also has Cannabigerol (CBG), Cannabinol (CBN) Cannabichromene (CBC), terpenes, flavonoids and essential amino acids making it the ultimate broad spectrum oil. Before we release any batch, it goes through rigorous on-site and third-party lab testing, and all test results are available on our website.

I find that CBD helps me deal with stress and anxiety, which in turn keeps my blood pressure where it needs to be. I've also been sleeping more soundly and wake up feeling rested. My sugar cravings are definitely less frequent which is an awesome bonus for a carbaholic. I feel that the CBD is a huge contributing factor with maintaining my weight loss. There is actual documentation about how CBD helps lower your food intake and lower sugar cravings–and I am living proof. It's amazing how it works with the body's endocannabinoid system to keep everything balanced! It has been such a gift and a miracle!

**Mindset and Maintenance**

Like everything, there are ups and downs when it comes to "maintenance". The past eight months have been a learning experience emotionally, physically, and mentally. From figuring out which foods work best for my body, to figuring out the psychological aspects of this whole lifestyle change. I'm learning that it's okay to indulge once in a while, but I find it fascinating how my brain perceives my appearance. If I make a less than perfect choice, I mentally "gain" all the weight back, instantly! For the most part, I still see myself as I was at 285 pounds. It is taking a very long time for my brain to catch up to my body, but I am getting better. I think the CBD is helping with that as well. Some days I have to remind myself that I fit into much smaller clothing and that there is no way I still look like I did 100 pounds ago. When I catch myself lost in those low moments, I think about how good I now feel, but sometimes I find a physical reminder snaps me back to reality faster. I have a piece of ribbon that I have cut to the length my waist measured at the beginning of this journey. I wrap it around myself so I can experience how much smaller I am. It really helps remind me just how far I've come. I'm proud that I took a chance on myself and knew deep down that I could do this.

I made the choice to take control of my health and it was easy once I focused on me. Every day is a series of choices, and I've learned that you don't have to be perfect to succeed, you just need to do your best to make the better choice! Life, like eating, is all about balance.

**ABOUT THE AUTHOR:** Jodie Penn is a multi-faceted woman. Her passions are family, art, helping others, and her two bulldogs—Brody and Layla. After years of working as a Creative Director in Corporate America, she left to partner with her mom to create AlphaZelle, a company dedicated to bringing the cleanest and healthiest products to the marketplace, including Nature's Golden Miracle brand of CBD, providing a trustworthy, natural source for vitality and empowered living. Jodie is a volunteer for Sparta Special Olympics focusing on their fundraising efforts and is a partner in Penn Creative Group, a design and development company, with her husband John.

Jodie Penn
Artist, Graphic Designer, Entrepreneur
Aplhazelle.com
NGM-oil.com
Jodie@AlphaZelle.com ~ 973-288-1971

# Spiritual Exam
## Wendy Luk

L ike many awakening journeys, mine began with a dark night of the soul. Everything in my life seemed to fall apart at once—my relationship ended badly, I got laid off from my job, and I was struggling with insomnia and depression. I didn't know what to do, where to go, or who to turn to. Lost, devastated, and seemingly alone, I had no idea that these traumatic changes were the Universe's way of pushing me toward my calling as an energy healer. Before I could embrace this role, I would first have to pass a "spiritual exam" to show that I had gained insight, inner strength, and comfort from my experiences. Imagine taking the most important test of your life, one that assesses all your fears, doubts, things you tried to escape in the past, and challenges you didn't overcome… all in one moment.

Seeking peace from the chaos in my life and relief from my insomnia, I took some group meditation classes. It was there that I learned of an energy healing course and was immediately intrigued. I signed up for the class, and just like that, I had met my first spiritual teacher.

After taking some weekend courses with her, I found out she was giving a two-week intensive where attendees would learn various healing techniques and be given a healing opportunity. My desire to go was soon overshadowed by mind chatter. Should I be spending the money right now? And what if I started a new job and I couldn't take the time off? Finally, I just said to the Universe, "If it is for my highest good and meant to be, please manifest this in my life." I no longer felt the need to figure out the how; I let go of being in control.

When I heard my teacher was looking for an assistant, I volunteered to help out for a few days. This worked out so well that she suggested a more permanent bartering arrangement—she would teach me in exchange for my assisting her, including at the two-week retreat! The Universe had answered my request and, I believed it to be a turning point in my life. *It's finally happening,* I thought, *I am stepping to my soul's calling to help others.* I felt so grateful for finding someone from whom I could learn and heal. I completely put my faith in her.

For the next year, I assisted her during classes and seminars, as well as on business trips, volunteer tours, and trade shows. At first it was all very exciting, however, I soon began to feel that something was not quite right. Instead of continually learning new things, it seemed I was repeating the same material over and over again, and I spent a lot of time doing chores completely unrelated to energy healing. In other words, there was a lot of assisting going on and not much mentoring. I also started to see a disconnect between the "spiritual teacher" persona she exhibited in class and the "behind the scenes" persona I saw once the students had left. Indeed, the more I learned about her personal life, the more I doubted the experiences she had recounted to me. I believed the healing events happened, but I wasn't sure exactly how. I would sometimes participate in a client's session and noted that when she later shared the healing experience it was different from the actual event. She exaggerated and dramatized the healing aspect of it.

She was a mass of contradictions, both personally and professionally. Her approach to teaching was "honest and straightforward"—sometimes to the point of bluntness bordering on offensive. She encouraged others to also "speak their truth"; however, she also thought she was right all the time and if anyone disagreed with her she assumed *they* had more inner work to do. It got to the point that others stopped raising issues with her because they knew she wouldn't listen. She taught trauma release, emotional release, and clearing multigenerational patterns, yet she was estranged from her oldest daughter and had unresolved trauma resulting from abusive experiences with her late mother. Her other daughter also had challenges and even attempted to take her own life. My teacher asked me to do healing work on her daughter, but she didn't realize that she needed some healing too.

I also found I didn't have much time for myself. She assumed and expected that I would always be available, and I didn't know how to say no. It felt similar to past relationships, in which I felt suffocated and like there were no boundaries between myself and the other person. I started to shut down and feel distant from her. I also did not feel well physically in her presence, experiencing fatigue and decreased appetite. My hair even started falling out.

The true turning point occurred during the third two-week retreat I assisted her with. I was in deep meditation when I heard the message that I was to confront her about offending people, as well as the tension with her daughter. I couldn't do it in private, as she would dismiss the whole thing before I even got started. Instead, I was to tell her during the three-hour workshop scheduled at the end of the retreat.

This was how the scenario unfolded during my meditation:

That last evening the group would form a circle, with me and my teacher sitting in the center. I would express gratitude for having the learning and healing experience with her, then address her issues with her daughter as well as her own need for healing and challenges around receiving love. I then envisioned everyone in the group opening their hands and sending love and healing to her.

I came out of the meditation unable to believe what I was being asked to do! Not only did I have to expose the challenges of a respected teacher, I also had to voice my opinions about her behavior. Most troubling, I had to express my own needs and risk conflict—in front of a group! These were all out of my comfort zone.

Here is what actually happened:

We did form a support circle that night, and my teacher and I were in the center. My heart was racing and my mouth was dry as I prepared to talk. After addressing some of my personal feelings, I broached the subject of her daughter, saying how much her daughter needed her, and that hurt and confusion was part of the reason she had attempted suicide. I also said that both the teacher and her daughter felt helpless and needed to heal the same issues. That's when my teacher cut in and accused me of being jealous and wanting to destroy her. With tears rolling down my face I tried to explain that I was trying to help, but instead of listening she just stormed out of the circle, waving her hands and saying " It's over! It's over!"

Clearly, this had not gone the way I envisioned!

Opinions among the group were divided. Some thought I had done the wrong thing; others thought I was speaking from the heart. *I* felt I had ruined the retreat for everyone. Devastated, depleted, and destroyed, I barely had the energy to go back to my room and fall on the bed. I wished I could go back in time and do it over. I wished I had spoken better. Most of all, I wished I hadn't done it at all!

For a while I lay there, frozen, unable to think, feel or cry. Finally, I phoned my friend (who is now my husband) to talk about what happened. He told me it had taken courage to do what I did.

"If you could do it over again," he asked, "would you do the same thing?"

At first it was hard to answer; it was still so raw. But when I really thought about it, I heard the answer loud and clear.

"It sucks and is so difficult," I said, "But if I need to, I would!"

We said our goodnights, then I lay face down on the bed. Suddenly, a feeling of calm came over me. My ears started ringing, and I felt a portal open over my head. I entered an altered state. I felt the Angel Realm coming through to me. I was told to remember all I had learned in order to heal myself from this situation. I understood I could release my trauma and rewrite the situation to create an alternate reality. Anything was possible. I took myself back to the event and rewrote the situation to reflect how I had imagined it, ending with loving, healing, and mutual understanding for me and my teacher, and an evening full of love and support for everyone. Instantly my anxiousness, sadness, and guilt were gone, replaced with love, harmony, and calmness. It was a complete one-eighty.

I also no longer felt the need to apologize to her, because I had done nothing wrong in the first place. Before, I had been dreading facing her and the class the next morning. Now I just wanted to hug everyone, and tell her of my experience. That night, someone slipped a note under my door. *You did your best,* it read, *With love and big hugs.* I took a deep breath in, thought to myself, *Yes, I did!* I was awestruck at how things had turned around.

The next morning, it was clear that my teacher did not want to talk to me, but I insisted, saying I would make it quick and that I wanted to thank her for the previous night. I told her I'd had an "A-ha" moment and experienced a quantum healing to release the negative emotions. This seemed to take her by surprise, but it changed nothing. She said there were people in her past who had tried to destroy her and bring her down. She also said my actions the night before had come from "my jealous and destructive side," and told me to work on it. She didn't seem to feel she needed to reflect on anything.

Before my breakthrough, I would have felt disappointed and angry; now, she simply didn't affect me. There was no trigger, just a feeling of lightness and liberation. That was a clear sign that I no longer needed to be afraid of my own ego and worry that I had an intention to hurt others. That had been my biggest fear, and an indicator that I didn't trust myself. Now that fear was gone. I had followed the instructions given to me by Spirit, and regardless of the outcome, that was enough.

She may not be the mentor I had hoped for, but she was definitely my teacher in many valuable ways. I learned I might become like her one day if I don't work on my ego. I learned to be kind to myself and to others, and not to take the people around me for granted. Most of all, I learned how to be humble and to keep striving to improve myself. Everyone is our teacher on our spiritual path, no matter if they hurt you or support you. They are placed in your life for a specific reason to help awaken you. This is the way the Divine works, bringing us lessons that feel challenging and painful until we are willing to see and accept the bigger picture.

The awakening process is not all roses and rainbows. Awakening means you are ready to acknowledge the lessons, missions, and challenges, and overcome soul trauma to break the vicious cycle. *Awakening* happens when you are no longer living in a dream world where you filter everything through your ego and focus on the future and the past. Instead, you have an almost simultaneous awareness of your individual self and the connection between that and everything else. Awakening is the process of moving from a fear-based existence to one based on love. It is a process of letting go of ego.

**ABOUT THE AUTHOR:** As an Awakened Lightworker, Indigo, and Starseed, Wendy's passion is to empower people to move forward and reach higher spiritual levels than they once believed possible. She specializes in clearing energetic blocks and trauma on the physical, mental, emotional, and spiritual levels, as well as in the auric and morphogenetic fields. Wendy offers an intuitive personal session to guide you to know your true self, to support your awakening journey, connect to your soul, and discover your gifts. She also provides free and monthly subscription-based healing to support your physical and energetic wellness. As a conduit of The Divine Energy, she has a gentle vibration through her healing to bring harmony between mind, body, and spirit.

Wendy Luk
Compassionate Healings
compassionatehealings.com
compassionatehealings@gmail.com

# CoThriving
*Weaving Community, Healing Earth Together*
Kathy Sipple

*"The future belongs to those who give the next generation reason for hope." ~ Pierre Teilhard de Chardin*

I meet my husband John in 1997, the day after my thirty-first birthday. Both of us have been married previously, neither have children. It's a long-distance relationship—he's in the Chicago Loop and I'm in Cincinnati. We proceed cautiously, intentionally, talking through preferences, including whether or not to have children. We agree we want a family.

When we finally marry, I'm thirty-six and he's forty-two. We settle on Valparaiso, Indiana as our new home. It translates to "Vale of Paradise" in Spanish. It's close enough for John to commute to Chicago for work and the schools are good. It feels like a great place to start a family. We also look forward to growing vegetables in our backyard and going for long walks on the many nature trails near Lake Michigan. Within me, the desire has been awakened to move beyond the paradigm of "I/me" to "we/us." I begin to feather our nest, to create a place of welcome for new life.

In the following years, numerous challenges to our health, careers, and finances ensue. I am now forty years old. My biological clock is ticking louder and yet it doesn't feel like the right time to start a family. John can see I am anxious and sad. One day he challenges me to go deeply within myself, to look for a path that will bring me happiness and best use my gifts. If I believe it is motherhood, then he says let's go for it, even if timing seems wrong. Letting go of anxiousness, I allow myself to remember a vision that came to me in my twenties and has since been nearly forgotten.

The rich details of the vision come flooding back. I see myself as a silver-haired elder in a culturally diverse, intergenerational community I have co-created with the other residents who live there. I am not related to them, yet we love and respect one another as family and we share a love of the nature that surrounds us. We gather around a fire to share stories and healthy food we have prepared together.

Re-membering this vision allows me to let go of my dream of becoming a traditional mother. I share with John that I instead intend to become a "Universal Mother" and that environmental projects in the community will be my children. Neither of us fully understands what that means at this point, but he is happy that I am happy.

## Web Designer

In 2009, I start my marketing consulting business, offering social media training and helping clients design strategies for building their social networks. The work is flexible enough and pays well enough to afford the opportunity to pursue other projects. I help launch an event called a Tweetup, a meetup for people who use Twitter and other social networks to learn to use social media and get to know one another in person. It's rewarding to see strangers become friends and share knowledge that's valuable to all. In my organizer role I find myself meeting more new people than ever before.

This group is tech savvy and capable of self-organizing. Once new leaders emerge, I step back and look for my next opportunity for community-building. Green Drinks, a monthly meetup with an environmental focus, needs an organizer and I volunteer. Though I don't have a lot of experience with environmental topics, I am fluent with online organizing tools and I know a lot of people to invite as speakers. Over the four years I run the program, I learn much from the presenters about our local food system, natural health, rain gardens, invasive species, watershed health, permaculture, green building methods, and so much more. I help nearby Michigan City and Gary start Green Drinks meetups of their own.

## Social Butterfly

I continue to build my network along with my knowledge. When I teach social media workshops I find myself integrating ecological metaphors to help students learn the concepts. I think of each new social media connection as a seed that, if nurtured, could become a beautiful thriving plant. And an expertly tended social network can provide a harvest of friendship, business opportunities, and knowledge. Recognizing that changing algorithms make it harder for a business to get its message across, I encourage "cross-pollination" as a marketing strategy, whereby likeminded entrepreneurs can work as allies, making the task easier and more enjoyable and yielding mutual benefits.

My environmental projects benefit from my expertise with social media. I look for ways to extend the reach of the presentations from the Green Drinks programs and decide to host some webinars and start a podcast and website I call 219 GreenConnect—219 is my area code and it's my intention to connect all the green people, ideas, and projects to one another through it. After a few years a group called Conscious Evolutionaries Chicagoland notifies me that I am to receive an award from Barbara Marx Hubbard for my podcast. Meanwhile, Earth Charter Indiana hears of my work and asks me to help organize my region around some sustainability initiatives leading up to Indiana's upcoming bicentennial celebration in 2016. It's a great opportunity to connect the network I am developing to areas beyond.

Interacting with environmental experts leaves me hungry to learn more. I sign up for every program I can: Master Recycler and Composter, Indiana Master Naturalist, Indiana Master Watershed Steward, Master Urban Farmer, mushroom identification classes, and permaculture. When each class ends, I attempt to keep in contact with classmates and sometimes collaborate on projects with them. I am invited to emcee Earth Day and it's fun to see so many people I know from different environmental initiatives all under one roof. How could we celebrate Earth Day every day, I wonder?

## The Wood Wide Web

*"Mycelium is the neurological network of nature. Interlacing mosaics of mycelium infuse habitats with information-sharing membranes. These membranes are aware, react to change, and collectively have the long-term health of the host environment in mind. The mycelium stays in constant molecular communication with its environment, devising diverse enzymatic and chemical responses to complex challenges." ~ Paul Stamets, Mycelium Running: How Mushrooms Can Help Save the World*

I love classroom learning but find many of my best ideas come when I am walking in the woods near the Indiana Dunes, especially if I quietly listen for answers from nature as I ponder a problem I'm trying to solve. I realize I have begun to feel like the Giving Tree in the children's book by Shel Silverstein. The book made me sad because the tree gave everything until there was nothing left to give. The boy who was supposed to be her friend never gave anything back.

I am frustrated when I am unable to answer a request for help in the ways most ask—serve on a board, build a website, volunteer at an event, teach a composting class. However, I regularly put the request to my network, taking time to match the need with the right person. As the broker in this transaction, my value added to the process is mostly invisible and unacknowledged. The more time I spend at it, the more I feel a need to create a different system to be more sustainable and to avoid burnout.

Dr. Suzanne Simard, a Professor of Forest Ecology at the University of British Columbia, has studied trees and discovered they have maternal instincts. While all trees in the forest are connected, the bigger, older "mother trees" serve as connection hubs and help younger seedlings grow by sharing their resources with them.

Inspiration strikes to develop a system of mutual support in my community. My research leads to timebanking, a method of exchanging services among members without using money. Unlike barter, any member can help any other member and "bank" their time to spend with any other member. I founded CoThrive Timebank in early 2016 in an attempt to make my otherwise invisible local environmental network visible.

## Timebank Growth Mushrooms...

*"Mushrooms were the roses in the garden of that unseen world, because the real mushroom plant was underground. The parts you could see—what most people called a mushroom—was just a brief apparition. A cloud flower." ~ Margaret Atwood, The Year of the Flood*

Our timebank software is called Community Weaver. The mushroom metaphor seems apt for timebanking—it takes a while for the mycelial threads to form into a visible mushroom. When the underlying network grows and more resources are shared among members, activity shows up like a fairy ring—a circle of mushrooms that expands as the underlying mycelium continues to grow outward, yet always remaining tethered to the host tree's roots.

As the founder and coordinator it is my greatest joy to help members see the value they offer to others. Many don't see their gifts as special or understand how others would benefit from them. Admittedly, when the network is smaller, exchanges are more difficult to broker as a ready match is not always available, but it gets easier.

The first few tentative exchanges are logged. People gather over a shared meal and learn more about one another's gifts. Friendships form. Trust grows. Social currency strengthens as people navigate this new way of interacting.

Some members are fearful they are "doing it wrong." Others accumulate time credits but are reluctant to spend them. Some resist the idea altogether, feeling it takes away from "pure volunteerism." Some are uncomfortable asking for help. I persist.

By our third year we attract some organizational members such as CommuniTree and NWI Permaculture. Organizations like these fit our members' interests perfectly since they are about planting trees and sustainable living. Our members are well-suited to help these organizations since many of them already have related skills to share.

We gain momentum as "guilds" form around a shared interest, seeing the mutual benefit they can offer one another by working in teams. These subgroups meet more regularly, independent of official timebank sponsored events. Their recorded exchanges become more regular and more frequent. Additionally, member pairs begin to form; they exchange services so often and so naturally that they "forget" all about timebanking and help one another now out of pure friendship, which is not a bad outcome though it makes measuring the true impact value of the network difficult.

In May members gather at a local nature preserve to remove invasive garlic mustard. In June a group forms around climate action. In August members fulfill support roles at a pop-up metaphysical expo hosted by another member. In September we host an Eco Skill Share where timebank members teach each other and also members of the public things like how to recycle properly, how to creatively upcycle items to avoid the recycling bin completely, how to identify wild edibles, how to remove invasive plants, how to collect native plant seeds, how to do Qi Gong, and more.

As 2019 comes to a close, our little timebank has exchanged over 2300 hours. The current value of a volunteer hour is given at $25.43, therefore our timebank's members have created nearly $60,000 of value if measured in the monetary economy. All of this on a shoestring budget and with no paid coordinator.

**Social Climate**

*"On a cultural level, we need to reintegrate human life with*

*the rest of life, and bring ecological principles to bear on social healing. On the level of strategy and thought, we need to shift the narrative toward life, love, place, and participation."*
~ Charles Eisenstein, *Climate: A New Story*

Mothering the timebank and its members has been my greatest honor to date. It is also, I believe, a model other communities can easily adapt and integrate to benefit their unique requirements and goals. It is my intention and vision to continue this life-affirming work, actively assisting these forward-thinking and connected communities to CoThrive so we can Heal Earth Together.

**ABOUT THE AUTHOR:** Kathy Sipple is available to help communities build resilience by offering training and support to launch and grow timebanking. She is working on a book, *Healing Earth Together,* expected to be published in 2020. The book will serve as a guide for communities to address environmental and social justice issues while enriching their own quality of life. Sipple holds a degree in Economics from the University of Michigan and is a member of Mensa. She lives in Valparaiso, Indiana with her husband John and their black Lab Bodhi. They enjoy frequent hikes at the Indiana Dunes State Park.

Kathy Sipple
Healing Communities By Unlocking Their Hidden Assets
linktr.ee/kathysipple
gatheringwithapurpose.net
kathy@cothrive.org

# La Luz Eterna
## Nicole Perez

I believe that before we are born our soul consciousness chooses what kind of incarnation we will have, including the lessons and experiences we encounter. Once we come here we also have a human consciousness, and while both are necessary for this journey, they are very different and often seem to be operating at cross purposes. Human consciousness involves an awareness of the mind and its surroundings; it is our perception of ourselves and the world around us. Soul consciousness has one objective: stay focused on your life purpose and do what you came here to do. When our human consciousness is disconnected from our soul consciousness, we suffer, we get sick, and we get lost in the drama of our human experience. However, when we are able to connect these states of consciousness through prayer, meditation, devotion, determination, and faith, we are able to access the wholeness of our Divine power. This awareness was one of the most important tools in my healing journey and helped facilitate my emergence from perpetual suffering and into my great life purpose.

My journey with illness began when I was just three months old. I was a colicky baby and, according to my mother, often cried uncontrollably for hours on end. It only got worse from there. At age two I had an emergency hernia surgery, and at age three I developed skin rashes from head to toe. When I played outside with other kids, my parents covered my arms and legs with hydrocortisone cream and wrapped me in saran wrap to keep it locked in place.

My dance with darkness began around age ten, when I developed an eating disorder. Anorexia is a dis-ease rooted in self-hate, and it led me to become my biggest bully. All day long I berated, judged, punished, and insulted myself for not living up to my rigid standards of perfection. My physical health declined rapidly during my teenage years, and by my early twenties I was drowning in a torrent of physical, mental, and emotional pain. My laundry list of medical diagnoses included endometriosis, polycystic ovarian syndrome, dysmenorrhea, adrenal fatigue, liver and kidney taxation, eczema, psoriasis, skin rashes and hives, GERD, irritable bowel syndrome, pre-diabetes, chronic sinusitis, hypertension, high cholesterol, asthma, life-threatening allergies, and advanced bone degeneration in my spine that caused chronic, debilitating pain. An x-ray revealed that the bottom curvature of my cervical spine had actually started to bend *backwards*. It quite literally looked like I was hanging myself, and that's because I was—mentally, spiritually, and emotionally. In fact, back then I had no spiritual beliefs or practices, and though I did not know it, I was also suffering with the pain of spiritual emptiness and disconnection from the Divine. It was my greatest core wound.

I saw countless physicians, all of whom were baffled by the severity and complexity of my illnesses. They didn't know what was happening to me, but they believed my conditions were irreversible. I was prescribed numerous medications that did not help the pain but did give me a host of awful side effects. I was angry. Angry at myself, at others, and at the world. Most of the time I didn't believe in God, the exception being when I needed someone else to hate. I had become lost in my own darkness.

I was twenty-five when I finally hit my breaking point. I had been bedridden for nearly two years and could not remember what it felt like to be pain-free. Now, in the rare moments I talked to God it was to beg for death so I could be released from my suffering.

One morning I awoke with a sharp, burning pain throughout my whole body that I had never felt before. It was so unbearable that I struggled to breathe. I crawled out of bed but was unable to walk and fell to my knees.

"Creator," I sobbed with my face in my hands, "please help me, I can't take this pain, I can't live like this… Please help me…"

It was the first time I had ever asked Creator for help. In that moment, time stood still and everything around me appeared to be moving in slow motion. It was a feeling of stillness, silence, and peace that I had never felt before.

And in that quiet, I heard Creator say to me, *If you are powerful enough to create this suffering, you are powerful enough to create the healing.*

As if someone had flicked a switch, something instantly began to change in me. I started to remember who I really was and what my purpose was. I looked down and saw a bright light coming out of the center of my chest, and an early childhood memory flashed through my mind. My mom was telling me the story of when I spoke my first words. At six months old I had looked up, pointed to a light in the center of the room, and said, "La luz! La luz!" (The light! The light!). Although I would not know it for many years to come, those precious first words contained the key to my true destiny.

The moment Creator first spoke to me was the most powerful of my life, and the beginning of my healing journey. In that moment I made a commitment to myself to become my own best friend instead of my worst enemy. I sat in front of a mirror, put my hands on my heart, and while looking into my own eyes, I began to apologize to myself. I apologized for all of the horrible things I'd ever said and done to myself, for all of the suffering I had caused, and for the suffering I had allowed others to cause me. I apologized to every organ, to my hair and skin, and to all of the parts of my body. I apologized to my heart, my mind, and my spirit. I forgave myself for not knowing any better at the time and promised that I would never insult myself again, no matter what. I made a decision to co-create my life with Creator in a way that was rooted in love, kindness, gentleness, and the heartfelt belief that I could turn things around.

I began cultivating spiritual practices that helped me to stay grounded in love and gratitude. I studied many different energy healing practices that I utilized in my own healing, and I found my life purpose as a healer and spiritual teacher. I began to heal from the inside out, and I learned that the most important relationship we will ever have is the one with ourselves.

My mental, emotional, and spiritual transformations were quickly followed by the healing of my physical body. Within a year I was off almost all medications and had healed nearly all of the dis-ease that had plagued me. New scans of my cervical spine showed that it had completely healed itself without any medical intervention. I was a living miracle, and I learned from Creator that miracles are not only possible for each and every one of us, they are our birthright.

My healing journey was not easy, but it was the training I needed to prepare me for a life of serving and guiding others with their own healing. I learned many important things along the way, the first being that when we find ourselves in a place where we are begging the Universe for swift and sudden death to end our suffering, we are on the brink of our greatest emergence. I learned that if we can find the strength to relax and breathe into the suffering instead of fighting it, we will begin to feel its impermanence. We will witness that in each and every second, it is passing, it is passing, it is passing. Learning how to be comfortable in the discomfort is no small feat, but it is a skill that serves us greatly in every area of our lives.

I say it again, our relationship with ourselves is the most important of our lives. Our thoughts, emotions, and beliefs matter; the way we talk to ourselves matters. When we are ill physically, the way we talk to our pain and disease matters. We should think of our thoughts and emotions as substances that we are feeding ourselves, because they quite literally are.

During my struggle with chronic pain I made a very important observation: if I told my pain how much I hated it, that it was ruining my life, and that my body was out to get me, it amplified immensely. On the other hand, engaging with my pain with love, care, and inquiry had the opposite effect. So I began to develop a very different relationship with my dis-ease. When the pain came, I would say things like, "I hear you, I'm listening to you, you have my attention and do not need to yell any louder. What's wrong? What is it that you need from me? What can I do for you?" I also started saying this mantra to my pain: "I love you, I'm sorry, please forgive me." I cannot emphasize enough how much this helped not only in decreasing the level of pain, but in turning the overall tide of my illnesses.

It's important to note that I did not find it effective to ignore the negative and say positive affirmations. This left me feeling inauthentic, like I was attempting a spiritual bypassing. Deciding to stop participating in destructive thoughts is an incredible commitment, and just because we make that commitment does not mean the thoughts will magically disappear right away.

Each time a negative thought fires, we have a decision to make. We can choose to participate in the thought, for example, by ruminating on all the reasons we are a failure and a horrible person. In effect we are choosing to feed the thought, and whatever we feed will grow in power. We can also choose not to participate. We can say to the thought, "I hear you, I see you, and I am choosing not to play with you today." In this way we begin to starve the thought, and whatever we starve will lose its power over us. This is how we begin to practice detachment, how we remain present with what is without getting hooked into the drama. We may inquire about the story of the thought to learn why it formed in the first place, with the understanding that we are not our thoughts or our stories. This is how we create space in the mind, rewire the brain, and create a new normal. It is where we begin to send a loud message to ourselves about what we are and are not willing to tolerate in our lives. This is absolutely critical in our healing.

By far, the most important thing that I learned on my healing journey is that everything we need is already inside us. *Everything.* Oftentimes we become too dependent on external sources to correct our dis-ease—not only conventional medicine, but energy healing practitioners and modalities as well. It is important that we seek help when we need it, but it is equally important that we fully participate in our own healing and aim to identify the source of the imbalance within us. Healers are not here to heal us; they are here to help us remember and awaken our own innate healing power. Our illnesses and pain often come to us as teachers, and it is important that we show up to receive the lessons they are trying to impart. If we bypass the lesson, it will come back around again and again until we are willing to receive it.

Each one of us contains the healing power of Creation within us. When we doubt ourselves, we are doubting the power of Creator. This is the power of love, and it is a matter of accessing it and aligning ourselves with it. This is often our greatest challenge, as it is easy to get hooked into the many distractions that we face on our human journey, but I am a living reminder that it is possible.

Come home to Love. Come home to Truth. We are all a living miracle, we need only to remember.

**ABOUT THE AUTHOR:** Nicole Perez is an indigenous woman from the Taino tribe in Cuba. An experienced healer and spiritual teacher, Nicole emerged from her own journey of chronic illness with a passion to help others do the same. She travels the country as a leader of sacred ceremony, and is also a singer of traditional Lakota ceremonial songs. In her private practice, ThunderHorse Healing, she helps people find and awaken their own healer within.

Nicole Perez
ThunderHorse Healing
thunderhorsehealing.com
nicole@thunderhorsehealing.com
773-366-2001

# Love Rush
## Linda Crea

The day was Thursday October 18, 2012. I was standing in my kitchen pouring a cup of coffee, just as I did every morning, when suddenly I felt a rich essence pour over me from above. It had a density to it and though I couldn't see it, I had a sense that it was white in color. It encompassed my being and radiated around me like a gentle rain, then filled me with something I would later describe as a "waterfall of love." I couldn't tell where it began or ended, yet I believe it continued to seep into the floorboards and beyond. I seemed to be channeling a surge of divine energy, and though it felt like a dream, I knew it was very, very real.

In that split second my life changed forever. As I stood there, coffee cup in hand, I caught myself wondering if I'd ever felt anything like that before. Was there something I dared to compare it to? Could it be measured to my love for my sons, any lover I had ever had, my friends, my horse or other pets? I was embarrassed to admit it, but nothing seemed to compare, not even in a small way. It was a "love rush" from high above, and I felt it radiate all around me, leaving me in a state of bliss.

I was nearly as amazed with the timing as the experience itself. Just weeks earlier I had made a personal vow to adopt a spiritual life-style and mindset so I could cling to God when people were making no sense at all. I was so determined to feel whole again that I had even enrolled in a spiritual healing course. Had my grand expansion happened because I'd finally opened myself up to getting some help?

You see, I had been through a tough few years and was exhausted by the aftereffects of a contentious divorce. My ex-husband and I had spent over ten years of an eighteen-year marriage in and out of counseling. I had tried my best, but by the beginning of 2009 I realized I could no longer pretend I was happy. Though I knew I would be met with harsh resistance, I finally dug in, mustered up my courage, and served him with divorce papers. I had no idea that I was about to embark on the toughest part of my life.

## Breaking Free - The Halt

For years I'd felt as if I were on a runaway horse. The same volatile scene would play out over and over in my mind—the horse, charging forward, out of control, while I fiercely leaned back, sinking deeply into the saddle, and screamed the word, "HALT!"

When he didn't stop, I would continue to press my heels down in the stirrups. I'd lift my hands up high and, with my hands firmly grasping the reins, pull back hard to make sure he knew I meant business. But he still wouldn't listen, he just continued to charge ahead with leaps and bounds. This horse had been on the run with me for a decade, but this was it; this time I was determined to stop him! I pulled my right rein in across his mane with great conviction and his head immediately swung to the right. I've got him now, I thought to myself. He was finally knocked off the powerful stride he was enjoying so much. Now he was paying attention to my commands and I was in control.

When he was still, all I heard was our hearts beating and the sound of our breath. And in this stillness, there was an underlying feeling of peace. He was exhausted and so was I. I was grateful it was over, and deep down; I believed he was too.

In reality, the "halt"—the end of my marriage—did not bring about peace or stillness. Instead, it would open the door to my dark night of the soul. In fact, for the next two years, there was not any part of my life that I recognized. I didn't have control over anything.

No one in our families wanted to see the marriage end. They knew we had been in and out of counseling for years and it was assumed that these appointments would continue "Until death do us part." I remember declaring, "Divorce does not mean death; it is an opportunity for new life for both of us."

No one was buying that theory, and about a year after the divorce was finalized, I found myself at the lowest point of my life. Unfortunately, when controlling family members with very strong personalities are involved in the marital affairs of others, words become daggers and people's feelings get hurt. Hurt is a broad understatement when you realize that these words cause not only emotional agony but physical pain as well.

I was also going through my own private despair. It's not uncommon for emotions to erupt to extremes during a divorce. So much rage and fighting occurs behind closed doors. Friends and family take sides; division of possessions and finances occur. Many find themselves blindsided by deceit, which opens the door to paranoia that never existed before. The children are understandably upset, which brings about another layer of loss and deep sadness. For anyone going through a divorce without compassionate support, it is overwhelming and may lead to physical consequences. Even if you are the one who asked for the divorce, it hurts a lot, and takes time to process all of it.

During those years, I found myself questioning why I had stayed in the marriage so long in the first place. I'd tried so hard during that decade of marital counseling, and now I wondered, who was I serving? Was it guilt over breaking the covenant of marriage, or my deep-rooted need to people please? In part I'd stayed for the sake of my children, but mostly it was because I never wanted to upset anyone; it was easier for me to stay miserable. I threw myself into my real estate career, but somewhere deep inside I'd known it was only a matter of time until the discord between me, myself, and I would cause my world to implode.

For the next two years I suffered in silence. My stomach was in knots and I had diarrhea every time I anticipated interacting with anyone from my past. I didn't want to encourage anyone to take sides, so I acted like I was as solid and strong as I had always been. At the same time, I realized I was severely burnt-out from my real estate career. Signs from the Universe made it very clear that it was time for me to get out of that business and find a new way of serving the public. Finally, I got the message and stopped trying to hold everything together. I slowly began to let go.

Was all of that part of the plan? Did I have to feel so suffocated and out of alignment with who I was in order to find my higher purpose? Were all of those characters and circumstances needed to help me get to where I needed to be?

The day that I confided to a friend just how much pain my stomach was in was the day I was pointed in the direction of God. That friend was a life coach and an energy healer, and as we spoke, I felt hopeful for the first time in years. That was when I signed up for the spiritual energy healing course and began meditating.

## Spiritual Gifts

Two weeks after I began the class, I experienced that "love rush" in my kitchen. This, I knew, was no accident. I had made a personal commitment to change, and I had asked to receive help from spirit. And oh, how Spirit had responded! My heart was now fully open to receiving more love and light than ever before, and I was ever so grateful that I'd been renewed. In time, I realized I could revel in this state of bliss anytime I wanted; I just had to ask. I called this asking, *prayer*.

Just over six months after my "love rush," I received a message regarding it. The message came to me through clairaudience. Clairaudience is a spiritual gift through which you hear words or have a visual imprint show up in your mind's eye. In my case I heard a jumble of sounds like *pasth, sir,* and *th*. They seemed to come from my higher consciousness or even another realm. I heard them a second time and then another—always short phrases that contained the same few sounds. I couldn't make any sense of the messages and would forget them within minutes of hearing them. The sounds would simply vanish!

Finally, I got smart and wrote them down before I could forget. It only took a few keystrokes on my computer, and the answer to my riddle was revealed. It was a Bible verse from Philippians 4:7 (KJV). It stated, "The peace which surpasses all understanding, keep your heart and mind through Christ Jesus." That was it! The love that was coursing through me was THAT! The feeling of love and peace that surged through me certainly surpassed all of my understanding. I realized humans don't often get to that high vibrational feeling of love and bliss. There is no way a human can be that loving all the time. It was something I had never realized before I began meditating.

Even though the verse came from the Bible, I knew it was the Universal flow of energy that comes from the Creator. I understood there were many different names for it. One may refer to it as the, Tao, the Universe, Source energy, or God to name a few. Call it what you like, but now I knew without a doubt what it was.

Now that I could channel that very high-vibrational energy, I felt incredibly fortunate. I knew I had it and I worked to keep it. That said, every one of us has the ability to channel this lovely energy. Jesus said, "Even the least of you can do what I have done." I take this sentiment to heart and through my spiritual coaching, teaching, and healing techniques open others to invite in a love rush of their own.

Since that astonishing morning, I have been on a prayerful journey full of gratitude that has brought me a myriad of blessings. I have learned that when making a decision, if you take a moment to ask your heart what it would do, all of your outcomes will be blessed beyond your expectations. You will also receive the feeling of the love rush as a reward every time you make heart-based decisions. Who wouldn't want that feeling of bliss to overcome them time and time again?

A spiritual lifestyle is not limiting in any way. It's a glorious place where patience exists and decisions come from a place of love. You will find you no longer have to be pushy and rushed in your life to acquire beautiful outcomes. It is a glorious convergence, where you and God are in constant communication, allowing you to attract and revel in everything you want.

It is indeed the kind of love that surpasses all understanding, and yet it is just the beginning of knowing how much you are truly loved, just for being you. Once again, I am overflowing with gratitude and love. Amen

**ABOUT THE AUTHOR:** Linda spent a few years stuck and cycling due to fallout from a painstaking divorce. When she realized she needed help, a whole new world opened up for her, one where she met God and adopted a lifestyle full of the glorious new spiritual practices she teaches today. As a certified spiritual energy healer, coach, and Ordained Minister, Linda hosts a variety of classes and services featuring: chakra clearing, chord cutting, prayer, forgiveness, and deep healing guided meditations. Linda is also the author of: By Grace ~ A positive path to wellness, and regularly posts inspiring vlogs that uplift and inspire.

Linda Crea
LindaCrea.com
instagram.com/lindacreaspiritualcoach
bit.ly/LindaCreaYoutube
facebook.com/SpiritualHealerLindaCrea

# Halo

### Saharai [Sara] Whaley

My awakening journey began during my quest to become a mother. Prior to having my son, I experienced five painful years of infertility. Five years of miscarriage after miscarriage, of undergoing every test and procedure known to Western medicine in order to find out why I could not hold life within my womb. Fortunately, Western medicine did not hold the answers that I was looking for. I say fortunately because this forced me to step outside my comfort zone and pursue other avenues. I refused to take no as my final answer or believe that my body was incapable of bearing a child (an obstinance I attribute to my zodiac placements). After two years of heartbreak and disappointment, I made the decision that I was going to release all the information that I had learned about pregnancy, the human body, and my overall belief system and start with fresh eyes. I was going to dive deep into the natural, spiritual, metaphysical, and esoteric studies I had been warned away from since I was a child. Reset, reboot.

This decision led me to incredible healers who held space for me and allowed me to explore my own traumas—including survival, control issues, and my need to please in order to be liked. During this process, I learned that in order to conceive and hold a child in my body, my own energetic vibration had to be strong enough to hold another's energy. As such, I was forced to identify and detach from everything and anything that was connected to me but did not belong to me. My biggest takeaway from my infertility journey was that I was not a body housing a spirit, but a spirit housing a body. My energy field was not only stronger than my physicality, it was also eternal, meaning it had been around long before this incarnation began and would continue to exist after it ended. These profound realizations led me to another: I had to shift my focus to nourish my spirit. When I accepted this as my truth, everything flipped, turned, changed, collapsed, and fell. I became pregnant and was able to carry my son to full-term.

After giving birth I thought I was in the clear, however, my soul had other ideas. It was not done learning. Being a mom was a lot more difficult than I thought it would be. I suffered from postpartum depression and was struggling emotionally, physically, mentally, and spiritually. I had done so much inner work to get pregnant and here I was once again losing all connection; I couldn't see past the anxiety, depression, and loneliness. Every breath felt heavy and suffocating, like I was experiencing a very slow-paced death, and the agony was magnetized throughout every vessel and cell in my body. Walking hurt, thinking was a nightmare, emotions were excruciating, and I felt like I had become a burden to my family. I felt like I had failed as a mother. My whole journey and the lessons I had learned all seemed like a sham.

One afternoon, I was sitting in my bed looking at my beautiful sleeping baby. My eyes flicked over to the mirror and saw the sadness in my eyes reflected back at me. My body, although physically fuller, felt empty. The TV was always on as background noise because I could not be alone with my thoughts. I was constantly contemplating how I had gotten to this moment. I felt like the more I learned, the more I realized I didn't know anything at all. And in this moment of pure defeat, I received a text from an old friend of mine whom I hadn't spoken to in years. She told me that she was learning to do energy healing, and while in meditation she had heard my name. She had heard that she needed to work on me.

I immediately texted back "Yes!" without knowing what the session would entail. I just knew that somewhere deep in my soul, I felt a flicker of hope. The next day, she came over and performed the first of many healing sessions on me. I could write a whole book on my incredible experiences with her; suffice it to say they led me to pursue becoming an energy healing practitioner myself.

During one of my energy classes, I was taught a healing technique called Heart Meditation. During this energetic meditation, the practitioner connects their own heart to the patient's heart while the patient is lying on a massage table. The practitioner then "spreads" the patient's energy field from the shape of a human body into that of a pancake-like platform. This allows the practitioner to zoom into the energy field and release the stagnant energy that is living very deep in the patient's chakras. Essentially, the process serves as an "energy microscope."

Like all healing techniques, this was taught and learned by working and practicing on one another in class settings. When it was my turn to receive the treatment, I laid down on the massage table and got comfortable with a pillow and a blanket. The lights were dimmed in the room and I quickly started to feel relaxed. Our instructor was playing soft instrumental music in the background.

The first thing I remember was feeling the practitioner's connection to my heart, first physically, then energetically. As the session progressed, my arms and legs slowly started to feel very heavy and dense. My hands started to tingle. It was a sensation not unlike that feeling a split second before a body part falls asleep. Imagine freezing that split second in time and having that sensation start to spread throughout your body like a sedative. Within minutes, I was covered in this "glittery" sensation and could no longer feel the table underneath me. I was floating. I felt an initial urge of resistance and discomfort rise inside my spine, an instinctual reaction of my body to fear and tension. *Survival*. I knew that I was safe and that I wanted to fully surrender to that moment of time and space. I also was aware enough to set the intention that I wanted to clear that survival vibration once and for all.

The next thing I remember was becoming aware of my breath. I couldn't feel air entering or leaving my lungs as it normally would. I knew that I was breathing—that was never a concern—but it felt different. I felt like I had entered a tank in which oxygen was circulating around me and my surroundings were breathing on my behalf to give me more space to fully surrender into the moment. The air around this tank felt cold and crisp. It felt lighter than air. So light in fact that it seemed that if the wind blew, the air would go right through me instead of around me.

I then felt an immense pressure build from the inside of my chest wall. I felt my ribs twitch slightly and then I released what seemed like an energetic explosion from my heart center. I was almost blinded by the beautiful neon emerald green color that suddenly appeared inside of me and all around me. From my studies, I knew that green was associated with the heart chakra, so I knew that my heart chakra had expanded massively and that I was floating in the midst of my own love. This was a powerful moment for me, and not just because of the obvious. Prior to this moment, I had never seen green. It was something that I had actively worked to attain because I believed that I could not hold healing space for others until I could see and experience my own love. I had to surrender my survival instinct in order to prove to the Universe that I trusted that it was holding healing space for me. And that trust came from self-love.

As the neon emerald green slowly subsided and turned into a golden misty light, I could see that I was in a white space that had neither a beginning nor an end. The golden light was circular in nature, a Halo, and it blended into the white background effortlessly. I was carried over to what seemed to be the threshold of the golden light and as I was placed over the beautiful spectrum of golden incandescent flakes, I heard the "music" and it took over all my senses. I use the word music because I do not have a better word to describe what I was hearing. It sounded like a symphony of singing instruments. I searched to find the source of the sound, but I couldn't. It was all around me. It sounded as if the songs were coming out from inside of me as well because I felt the vibrations of the notes swimming throughout my floating body.

The voices were singing in a language that I did not understand mentally, however, my emotional body seemed to understand every lyric. My emotions started to well up. All of them. It was a mixture of love, happiness, sadness, anger, past, present, future, and everything in between. It was as if the Universe had taken all the emotions I had experienced in every lifetime, mixed them in a blender, and poured them all over me. I know it sounds awful when I describe it in this way, but it wasn't awful; it was overwhelming in the most beautiful way. It was like being baptized by the angelic realm, with my own energy. I wanted to cry, but I didn't know whether I was happy, excited, scared, or sad. At the same time, I experienced immense gratitude for being able to feel all these emotions at once.

And then it hit me. Up to that point in time I had been privileged to live a life of ups and downs. Each roller coaster ride, each up-side-down curve, each free-falling moment that I had ever taken were all proof that I was worthy of living because I was feeling all of it. I had a purpose just by being alive. Yes, the process was emotionally, mentally, and spiritually draining. But in the end, we are here to create, and in order to do so we must learn how to feel, acknowledge, let things die, fall off, and renew. And we must also accept that life doesn't always present under the best circumstances.

I cannot tell you with exact accuracy how long this event was in human time, but I would estimate that it was about fifteen minutes. As I started to come back into my body, the music became less and less intense and the vibrations and tingling within my body started to subside. I felt the air entering and exiting my lungs again. I also felt the table beneath me. I was fully present and back in the room.

If you are reading this, you are likely going through something very personal that is confusing and scary. If there is anything that you can take away from my story, it is that you are never alone. You are always guided, held, and more importantly, are receiving love from realms you don't even know exist. That day I received confirmation from the heavens that there is an angelic realm. Prior to this, I had never given it any thought; in fact, I had never believed in angels at all. But that didn't matter because the angels believed in me and even though I was far from my best, they chose me to experience this beautiful retreat of light, hope, love, and magic so that one day, I could extend the same magic to you. The Universe awakened me to this reality so that I could one day hold healing space for others on their path to "Woke."

**ABOUT THE AUTHOR:** Sara Whaley is an energy healer and modern-day medicine woman with the ability to connect one's energy blocks to their physical ailments, and the understanding that this energy must be acknowledged and validated before it can be transmuted from the body. Sara sees and feels these energy blocks as clearly as if they were physical objects; she can also discern whether they are from this life or a previous one. These gifts, along with her unique, heart-centered combination of modalities to cleanse auric fields, balance chakras, eliminate energetic blockages, release stagnant energy, and integrate new energy make her a healing powerhouse.

Saharai [Sara] Whaley
Third Eye Metamorphosis
thirdeyemm.com
sara@thirdeyemm.com
Intagram: @thirdeyemm

# For Every Season, A Purpose
## Ann Franzese

In examining my life I have come to notice a pattern in which I periodically take stock of the many hats I have worn and those I still have yet to wear. Within each season, the same two questions emerge: "What is my purpose?" and "Am I living it to its fullest potential?" Each attempt to answer these questions has led to a-ha moments I call "awakenings."

The first such awakening occurred when I was a teenager and considering what my next step was after graduating high school. In our family the highest values were placed on education and Christianity—education was seen as a path to a better life, and Christian beliefs served as the foundation for that life. My dad was the first in his family to go to college, and my early years were spent in married student housing at the university he attended. My mother held down the fort at home, caring for him as well as me and my sister. I realized that just as college had provided my parents with a way out of their blue collar community, it would now provide me with opportunities that were unavailable to my mother and so many other women of her generation, namely personal and professional autonomy.

Indeed, my college years were particularly instrumental in the development of my confidence and independence. Toward the end of my freshman year, the arrival of The World's Fair in my college town brought with it not only excitement but an influx of jobs that afforded myself and many others the opportunity to work and live on our own over the summer.

It was a big leap to not go home, yet I couldn't pass up the chance to gain some work experience and meet people who wouldn't normally cross my path. The following summer I did return home, only to find myself bored without my friends and earning far less money than I had at the Fair. This encouraged me to spend the remaining summer at school and move forward in my personal growth. I also worked during the schoolyear, and after graduating I took my savings and joined two friends on a trip to Europe. We travelled to ten countries in six weeks, our itinerary directed only by our Eurail Pass, the travel book *Let's Go Europe,* and our sense of adventure. There were many highs and a few pretty big lows that required us to adapt and change course, always growing and learning along the way. If we had the strength to navigate these changes in countries where we couldn't speak the language, imagine what we could do in our own country, even outside the comfort of our home states!

This sense of adventure stayed with me as I flew from London back to Knoxville, TN, and after a few days I was packing up my things again, next stop: Chicago. One of my former roommates had already been living there for a year and she loved it. She thought I would too. Living in the Windy City would prove to be as exciting as Europe and even more challenging as I pounded the pavement armed with little practical experience but a desire and a dream. It turned out to be enough: I found part-time work that first weekend and, three weeks later, a full-time job. That job, while a bit rough the first year, proved to be fulfilling both mentally and financially. I was working for a Fortune 500 company known for its excellent sales training program. This company became my second family as I forged a sales management career path, developing both individuals and teams. The long hours we put in paid off; my team and I honed our strategies and attracted company recognition, earning annual achievement trips and surpassing financial goals. At the age of twenty-seven I bought my own condo. Life was good!

I experienced another shift while attending graduate school. I was now married with a new baby, who arrived right after the first year of school. Three weeks after my son was born, I jumped back into school so that I could finish the program with my original classmates. The demands of a new baby, work, school, and marriage had me both emotionally and physically drained, and left me and my husband asking ourselves how we could and should raise our family and build a balanced life. In the end, I decided to leave my job and focus on school and motherhood. Our second child, a daughter, arrived three months after my graduation ceremony. We had entered into a new season of life, building our future as a family.

And that we did. We were able to live in a fabulous community and even built our own home. Our life centered around immediate and extended family and friends. Our children flourished and participated in sports, dance, theater, church, scouting, and more. My husband had his sport and I was able to perfect mine along the way too. As life got busier, traveling became a priority and a sacred time for our family to enjoy each other away from the demands of daily life. Life was better than good, but as they say, all good things must come to an end.

My biggest awakening came not in the form of an adventure or epiphany, but as an emotional explosion that shook me to my very core. It was like a volcano, slowly and quietly building pressure until one day, seemingly without warning, it erupted, destroying everything in its path. For us, that underground pressure were those ever-increasing demands of the life we had built. They left me and my husband feeling drained and unable to understand each other's position. Even parenting ultimately became divisive, as did other decisions. What was once an attitude of cooperation now had become an attitude of right versus wrong. As the pressure mounted, I became increasingly unsure of myself with regard to my role in the marriage, often feeling undermined or not good enough.

After what I now realize was a half-hearted attempt at therapy—meaning we didn't stick with it long enough to reap any benefits—we decided to divorce. Several years later, we would learn just how good therapy can be through the experience of our daughter.

The dissolution of our marriage was far more rancorous than I ever could have anticipated. Though it took two and a half years to obtain the divorce decree, we would spend eight years in litigation. First, someone wanted to change the agreement, which extended the process another year and half; then there were the instances of noncompliance to that agreement that brought us back to court time and time again. In total, there were over four hundred fifty petitions recorded, and considering the cost of a petition, it became glaringly apparent that the only winners in this game are the lawyers. This of course took an enormous toll on everyone, especially our kids, who were then still in high school. I understood then what my friend meant when she described going to the courthouse as "going to the sewer." It feels ugly and raw to be fighting over seemingly trivial (but actually quite important) issues in front of a bunch of strangers.

One of the first recommendations many divorce lawyers make to their clients is to engage a therapist, and anyone who has taken part in this process would probably agree. It is an emotional roller coaster that often reveals the worst aspects of the person you once considered a partner, not to mention your own. It was the only time in my life that I experienced panic attacks. At first I likened them to being allergic to my cat, yet I soon found that these eruptions coincided with certain events. Now I knew why my son got stomachaches when he didn't understand his seventh-grade homework and feared getting a bad grade.

I have often been told that God works in both the valleys and the mountains. His best work is in the valleys, as that's where the faith and growth come from. Our legal wrangling has definitely been one of the deepest valleys, but it has been essential to uphold the agreement we finalized in 2013. It remains essential to this day, not only for my benefit, but for my children as well.

My divorce, though incredibly painful, has brought about the greatest transformation of my life. It was my opportunity to invest in myself and start building a new career opportunity that aligns with my wants, needs, desires, and my purpose.

During my family's unhinging, I sought out and began this next journey by asking myself those tried and true questions: What do I want to be when I grow up? What will my next chapter entail? How do I want it to look? What's important to me today? Bridging my desires and my past experiences and interests in personal development, I took a deep dive into the coaching world. There, I continued to learn even more about myself and how my thoughts, experiences, and beliefs have shaped my choices. I have also learned how I can continue to make choices that create greater possibilities for me, rather than closing doors. This idea of conscious awareness, the ability to hone in on our emotions and elect how we want to feel versus being at the mercy of those feelings, is one of the most empowering tools we can master to build a life of joy and happiness.

As we travel through life, we find ourselves traveling in the footsteps of others, usually our parents, grandparents, and other elders. We accept their age-old adages with regard to everything, including how we view ourselves, our mistakes, the world, and life in general. These inherited perspectives can leave us feeling open and willing to unite, be in community, and listen to our hearts, or they can leave us feeling fearful, anxious, stressed, and living in avoidance, dissonance, and judgement, closed off to our dreams and possibilities. The point is, whether they are positive or negative, they are based on the biases and beliefs of others, and as we mature, we must regularly assess them to make sure they align with the person we want to become or are becoming.

Today, I am in my wisdom season in many areas of my life which allows me to share and mentor as a coach. At the same time, I am a novice in other areas and am excited to explore those uncharted waters with passion and purpose.

My greatest takeaway is that we can be anything we want to be IF we can learn to see beyond our ego and be open and aware of how and why we do what we do.

Just as I have had to find my power over and over, I challenge you to lean into your power, to find it or reignite it, so you too can open the doors to your own possibilities, fulfill your dreams, and build even bigger ones along the way.

As Glinda the Good Witch tells Dorothy in The Wizard of Oz, "You've had the power all along, my dear. You just had to learn it for yourself."

**ABOUT THE AUTHOR:** Ann is a leading authority in helping others cultivate emotional intelligence and shift their thinking to open doors to new possibilities and dreams. She has over twenty years of experience in the corporate sector, specifically sales/sales management, performance, business and organizational development, team-building, leadership, and succession planning. She has also served on the boards of non-profits, with roles in operations, major capital campaigns, organizational design, and fundraising. In addition to degrees from the University of Tennessee and Northwestern University, Kellogg Graduate School of Management, Ann holds coaching certifications from the International Coaching Federation, the Institute of Professional Excellence in Coaching (IPEC) and the CreatingWe Institute. Ann resides in the Chicago suburbs with her son and daughter.

Ann Franzese
Executive Coach
journeytosuccess.me
ann@journeytosuccess.me
Quiz: assess.coach/journeytosuccess

# Free To Be Me
## Dr. Jo Anne White

I believe we can have more than one a-ha moment that shakes us up and shapes our lives. They lead us in different directions and onto new pathways. These are turning points when our perception shifts and we can see ourselves and our lives in a novel way. The next course is to act: Undertake the task of following through to be in alignment with what feels right to us and opens us even more to our purpose and what we're here to do.

For me, one such turning point, and a true awakening, happened after a dancing injury. I was seeking medical help to heal my knee and myself, return to full function, and maybe even dance again. I was seeing different physicians, yet the pain continued to worsen. I had trouble getting around and doing normal daily activities that we often take for granted like walking and sitting. A physician recommended a technique to strengthen my knee but instead it pulled out my lower back, creating even more discomfort and injury. When climbing the stairs to my bedroom became too difficult to maneuver I was forced to sleep on the uncomfortable couch downstairs, thus adding fatigue to my list of ailments. It was a dark and lonely time for me. I was depressed and hopeless and admittedly feeling sorry for myself too. It seemed there was no end in sight to what I was going through. Just one day without pain and limitation would have been a precious gift.

One night I had a dream that infused me with a resurgence of new faith and the energy to heal myself. I dreamt I was lying on an operating table in a white room with several beings dressed in white robes gathered around. No words were spoken; they just stood silently over me, radiating a beautiful white light. They weren't operating, yet they were healing me with their hands and energy. Throughout the dream I felt a calmness overtake me.

For some, that dream might have evoked a creepy feeling or troubling thoughts, but not me. Instead, I awoke feeling more energized, optimistic, and encouraged by what I had experienced. Rays of hope surfaced. Maybe I would finally get the help that I needed and be healed. At the very least, I'd be better than I was. The belief that I could find answers to heal my injuries and that I would feel and be whole again resurfaced. It was as if the light of those beings had penetrated my darkness.

With renewed strength, I sought out alternative ways of healing including hypnosis, the Alexander Technique, energy healing, chakra balancing, meditation, sound healing, and much more. Through these new methods and techniques, I not only became healthier and stronger, I studied and became certified in several of them. Initially it was just to help myself heal, however, I believe I'm always guided. Somehow there was more in store for me and more reason to study them, though this didn't emerge with clarity until later on.

Fast forward several years. I was completing my doctoral dissertation and working as the Executive Director of the comprehensive Children and Youth Services Program for Bancroft, Inc. which encompassed school, residential and community living, vocational training, parent and teacher training for individuals with special needs, and much more. I was blessed with a dedicated team and believe we did wonderful things to serve the children and youth and their families. My heart was beautifully engaged.

Then the organization underwent a restructuring. The three executive positions, including mine, were dissolved, and I was offered the position of Director of Research, Evaluation and Training, which encompassed not just the Children and Youth program but the Adult Programs as well. It was an esteemed, enormous promotion, and a recognition of my efforts which included opening community living opportunities, State certification for our vocational program, creating financial solvency, and published research.

This appointment was surely an honor, and with a committed team much good came from it. Yet something was missing. I had begun to do other workshops and trainings for people outside of the education and special education arenas and was feeling a strong, insistent pull in another direction. At that time I was also teaching an evening class at Temple University, and as I walked from my car to my class, a billboard advertising some alcoholic beverage would catch my eye. It was not the advertisement, however, but the message—"Do what you love and the rest will follow"—that jolted me and captured my attention. Each time I viewed it, my eyes would well up with tears; something happened to me internally.

Somehow that billboard message upturned all that I had presumed to be my destiny and my future. Initially I was deeply engaged and focused on serving the children and youth and their families, but my new position lacked the close connection that had drawn me there in the first place. My insides were beckoning me to do something else, something more. I felt a persistent calling and an urge to move into the unknown and embrace a new future.

Seeds were being planted and a soft voice inside asked me what's next. The alternative methods that I had studied and used to heal myself were working well. I was even dancing, not professionally, but dancing! Other messages followed that led me to feel more confident about using my knowledge and certifications to serve others. If I was being helped on so many levels, wasn't it not just possible, but responsible, for me to utilize my skills to help others too? The answer was a resounding Yes! It didn't happen immediately, but the promptings got louder and more insistent.

With both fear and excitement, I finally gathered the courage to turn in my resignation. Since I had an important position, I had to give two months' notice, two months during which I wondered and questioned whether I was up to the task of being self-employed and doing something entirely different than ever before. Yet my doubts were silenced by my faith that I was being led. During that time I experimented and began holding workshops that drew people to my messages and to new ways of healing and becoming healthier physically, emotionally, mentally, and spiritually.

I didn't share my plans with my family until much later, probably because I didn't want anyone to discourage and deter me from my goal. This surely felt like the right next move. They believed my job was respected and prestigious, and it was, but that just wasn't enough for me. The day finally came and with both hope and misgivings, I said my goodbyes. I was honored with a farewell dinner for my service and achievements. When it was time to leave, I walked out, so grateful for the time I had spent, the people, and all I had learned and been able to accomplish. I was free to start the next chapter of my life!

In hindsight, I probably didn't prepare myself amply for going out on my own, yet I did anyway. I received certifications in business and personal coaching and combined them with my previous knowledge base to create programs and seminars, as well as group, family, and individual sessions. It's wonderful when we're being encouraged, propelled and directed to make fresh choices that open us to new ways of being while also expanding and growing ourselves and our abilities. I love what I do and enjoy helping others. It's a rewarding life choice and one I believe wasn't accidental. Although I had to go through trauma and drama, it led me to a new calling and to more of myself. To this day, I derive much satisfaction from watching the people I work with thrive with more inner confidence, success, and wellbeing in all areas of their lives. I also love to teach others how to connect with their soul's guidance and inner resources to help them live and work more fully and joyfully.

To me, the most beautiful takeaway from the shifts I underwent is the opportunity for self-expansion. My injury led me to self-healing and to a new way of helping others and enhancing lives, including my own. My experience at Bancroft taught me so much and I believe I truly made a difference there too. What's also wonderful is that I still work with atypical individuals and their families and have been a staunch advocate in education and other arenas to ensure life and work engagement, enrichment, acceptance and respect for all.

We are here to awaken to our expansive selves, uncover and utilize our gifts and refine them. Running from them, afraid of their power and how they will disrupt our lives, can have unpleasant and even unhealthy consequences.

One of my clients had the gift of psychic ability from a very young age. This gift terrified her so she stifled it and stuffed it down deep inside. Believing that what she was experiencing wasn't "normal," she told no one, not even her parents or her sister. The internal conflict she created by not honoring her ability left her not only immobilized with fear but physically sick as well.

Her doctors couldn't find anything wrong with her, but she was drained, lacking energy and drive, feverish most of the time, anxious, depressed, and in constant pain and distress. It was as though she had become imprisoned by her fear and inaction. With my support, she finally accepted her gifts and learned how to use and master them so that she wasn't overwhelmed or controlled by them. It seemed miraculous, yet the more she embraced her talents, the healthier and happier she became. Soon her energy and vitality awakened. She was able to work and feel better about herself, her gifts, and her life and share them with others.

Oftentimes we doubt ourselves and don't believe in our worth and in our own abilities. A strong nudge from within and external help can shift our belief and open us up to unimagined miracles and possibilities. A former client of mine was weary of corporate life and wanted to start her own company. She had the expertise, energy, resources, and the respect and connection of many, however, she was stifled by a lack of belief that she could do it and flourish. Then she received an out-of-the–blue message from an old colleague.

When they spoke she found out that her friend was also interested in venturing out on her own. The timing of the call, their strong collaborative bond, and encouragement and belief from me validated her inner desire. She began to believe her yearning was not just a whim, but a genuine aspiration beckoning her. Their business and partnership commenced and soon took off. She later admitted to me that she was never happier or as successful.

Our awakenings can be small moments of clarity or colossal events that shake us to our core and transform us. They can unearth new pathways in our journey and offer greater opening, understanding, and acceptance of our more expansive selves. They may arise from catastrophic situations, enlightening moments, messages, and synchronicities steering us into realms and outcomes never considered before. What's most rewarding is to not only recognize the calling, message, and the magnetic appeal, but to pursue it. This can require a leap of faith, often without a safety net. Sometimes we need to take that leap with determination and trust and be "Woke"! I'm thankful that I did.

**ABOUT THE AUTHOR:** Dr. Jo Anne White is an International #1 bestselling, award winning author, speaker, and consultant, recognized as a Goodwill Global Ambassador for civil and humanitarian work in education, entrepreneurship, coaching, and women's issues. A certified life, spiritual, and business coach, and energy master teacher, she empowers and inspires men, women, families and businesses to achieve greater health and wellness, master success, thrive, and triumph. Executive Producer and Host of the POWER YOUR LIFE Shows, White's been featured online, in publications such as Good Housekeeping, More, and WebMD and appeared on Radio and Television Networks such as NBC, CBS, FOX and Voice America.

Dr. Jo Anne White
Dr. Jo Anne White Coaching and Consulting Services
drjoannewhite.com
joanne@drjoannewhite.com
856-795-5854

# Chemical Free From A to Z and CBD

Dale Schock

*Oh my God, I can't breathe—am I having a heart attack?* There's pressure on my chest, my heart's racing, and everything around me looks foggy. Sick to my stomach and dizzy, I'm also sweating profusely.

I'm terrified! Only twenty-four years old and these strange symptoms come upon me when I'm driving my children home from a routine doctor visit.

Subsequently I find out that I experienced an anxiety attack. Soon, I begin feeling anxious and fearful more frequently, particularly when leaving my house. The only place I feel truly safe is in my own home.

Eventually going out is not even an option for me and, as the years go by, my anxiety attacks increase. I begin to make excuses to explain why I don't attend my children's school functions, visit with friends and family, or go grocery shopping,

The truth is that I've become housebound, and the doctor diagnoses me as agoraphobic!

Five years after my agoraphobia diagnosis—essentially a fear of being in open or public places—I'm basically a hermit. Until...I decide to take back my life! With the help of family and friends, I'm able to overcome my anxiety, and slowly I rejoin the living. What a relief!

Finally, just as I seem to have gotten back to normal, I begin to experience pain in my abdomen and bleed so heavily each month that I'm stuck in my house for a week. When the pain gets so bad in the middle of each month that all I do is lie in my bed and cry, I decide it's time to visit the doctor.

Diagnosed with ovarian cysts and fibroid tumors, the cysts are so large the doctor is afraid they may be cancerous. I'm told I need a hysterectomy. My scheduled surgery that's supposed to take two hours lasts for five. I find out later that not only do I have huge tumors and cysts, but also endometriosis, which complicated my surgery.

Recovery from the hysterectomy is difficult. By now I'm forty and my hormones, or lack thereof, wreak havoc on my body and my emotions. Prescribed hormone therapy simply doesn't work; I stop taking it and hope for the best.

## The Common Denominator

A year after my hysterectomy I start to notice rashes all over my body. No matter what I do, they won't go away! Within months my body is one giant oozing, itching, painful rash! Unable to tolerate even the most comfortable clothing, or lie down in bed, my doctor diagnoses me with *contact dermatitis* and prescribes a steroid and an antibiotic.

Three rounds of treatment later and still I find no relief! I learn that when a doctor doesn't know the cause of a rash, he or she labels it *contact dermatitis*. Not satisfied with simply treating my symptoms, I want to understand *why* this is happening to me! Once I identify the cause or causes, then I can eliminate them!

I look back over the past twenty-five years and wonder if my agoraphobia, hysterectomy, and skin rashes can possibly be related. Perhaps what makes me sick has a common denominator! I start by listing all the things with which my skin comes into contact on a daily basis. I'm surprised to discover that—on an average day—I encounter over five hundred different chemicals!

I used hand wash, shower gel, shampoo, deodorant, body lotion, bar soap, toothpaste, hair styling gel, perfume, eyeliner, mascara, makeup, and lipstick—all personal care and household products— and all before breakfast! Then there's the dishwashing detergent, window and household cleaners, disinfect for the bathtub, toilet, and sink, and more...

It's unbelievable how many different chemicals my skin comes in contact with every day!

They say a little knowledge can be a dangerous thing. All this time I assumed that our skin is an impermeable protective barrier that keeps the good stuff in and the bad stuff out. I couldn't have been more wrong, as my research shows that our skin absorbs whatever substances—good or bad—come in contact with it!

Additional research leads me to realize that all these products contain toxic chemicals that *denature* protein. This means that these toxic chemicals modify the molecular structure—especially via heat, acid, alkali, or ultraviolet radiation—of a protein or DNA, so as to destroy or diminish some of its original properties.

In short, these toxic chemicals change how we look, and not in a good way, by increasing the appearance of age spots, brown spots, wrinkles, sagging skin, and puffy eyes. In addition, they can cause a plethora of ailments—including hormone disruption, joint pain, skin reactions, allergies, depression, headaches, chest pains, ear infections, chronic fatigue, dizziness, loss of sleep, early puberty, hyperactivity, irritability, behavioral changes, violent coughing, vomiting, cancer, heart attacks, blindness, and even death!

What a frightening *aha!* Moment it is when I realize everything my skin comes in contact with that can affect my life so dramatically. It turns out my medical issues have been caused by a combination of chemical toxins built up over an extended period of time. This causes a breakdown in my immune system and hormone disruption.

Suddenly, the fact that I started menstruating at eleven and had a thyroid problem makes sense, as both are hormone related. All those bubble baths and all that tooth brushing creates hormone disruption! Bubble bath liquids and toothpaste contain substances such as sodium hydroxide—which is the same as lye!—triclosan, a pesticide, and propylene glycol, or anti-freeze.

In addition, I discover through my research that, since 1938, the U.S. government does not regulate or control what's used in cosmetics sold in this country. That means products may contain *any* chemical substance and manufacturers are *not* required to list them as ingredients.

## The Solution: AlphaZelle to the Rescue

Now that I know I'm chemically sensitive and have severely damaged my skin, my first job is to eliminate toxic ingredients from my life. I begin by going through all my products and boy do I have a rude awakening! Every single product I use has toxic chemicals in it—with no exceptions!

By this point I've learned that *chemical sensitivity* and/or *toxic overload* eventually damage our alpha, or *mother,* cells—situated at the very base of the skin. These cells are responsible for periodically forming new skin cells which replace the dead cells that slough off on a daily basis.

As damaged alpha cells send increasingly more damaged new cells to the surface of our skin, these unhealthy cells eventually become fine lines and wrinkles, brown or age spots, sagging skin, puffy eye bags, and many other embarrassing skin conditions.

I realize my rashes will *never* clear up unless I repair my deep alpha cells. For me to get healthy and address my problems I need to use products with *no* toxic chemicals in them.

My search for safe, non-toxic products begins, but despite looking in health food stores and natural companies, I find no totally clean products. Even the ones labeled "natural" or "organic" include chemicals and fragrances!

Eventually I realize the only way to guarantee what's in the products I use is to formulate my own!

During my research, I'm fortunate to develop a relationship with a few cosmetic chemists willing to work with me. They help me experiment with powerful and safe active ingredients, and to develop toxin-free preservative systems that will have a long shelf life.

We begin to develop products that perform as advertised, feed the skin with proper nutrition that accelerates healing, and repairs the mother/alpha cells that are toxically overloaded. We start with a few products that can help as many people as possible, including a hand wash, shower gel, shampoo, conditioner, body lotion, facial cleanser, and facial moisturizer.

I name our company AlphaZelle—Alpha for "first" and Zelle for "cell," because this is where real health truly begins. Over the years, we're able to fine-tune our products and use the safest, most powerful active ingredients. Now, after ten years, we have over sixty different "clean" products that don't cause hormone disruption or immune system issues.

Unfortunately, I will probably always be *chemically sensitive,* even though my alpha cells continually heal and constantly send healthy new cells to my skin's surface. However, I can't remember now the last time I had a headache, lacked energy or ambition, or experienced rashes, since my skin has responded so well after many years of feeding it the proper nutrition that our products provide.

I now know how important it is to live a toxin-free life—I only wish I'd learned this earlier!

It's become my mission to educate others so that they and their children don't experience the kind of torment and confusion I did. The most important thing I learned is that I must read ingredient labels. Since our skin absorbs everything it comes in contact with, all ingredients should be as pure as the food we eat.

If I don't think I'd eat it, I won't put it on my skin! I'm profoundly aware that some companies don't want me to know what's in their products and will cleverly disguise toxic ingredients by combining them into a "proprietary blend" with a name I cannot identify or rename an ingredient to make it sound safe.

Also, companies are not required to disclose the chemical makeup of fragrances, or to list impurities or contaminants. If an ingredient list causes any doubt, I err on the side of caution and keep looking for a cleaner product. I formulate my products with therapeutic food grade essential oils instead of synthetic fragrances.

## From A to Z comes CBD

Being involved in the 'Alternative Health' field for more than half my life, I am always interested in new and innovative products. One day my friend approached me and asked if I had heard of CBD and what did I think of it? The interesting thing was that I had been researching CBD for a while and I was totally amazed by all the health issues it addressed including ADHD, anxiety, arthritis, depression, inflammation, chronic pain, stress, PTSD, and sleep to name a few. I purchased a couple of different CBD products to try, and bottom line: I only felt a difference from one of them.

After educating myself further, I found that not all CBD is the same and this industry was just like the cosmetic industry with no regulations. I knew I wanted to provide these incredible benefits of CBD to our customers, and I decided the only way I could have a CBD product that I could trust and believe in, was to have my own product line that I had full control over. I named our company 'Nature's Golden Miracle' because it comes from nature, it's golden in color, and I consider it's many benefits a miracle!

Nature's Golden Miracle is created from a unique propriety strain of medicinal hemp that is naturally high in cannabinoids. Our CBD is formulated with THC-FREE Phytocannbinoid Hemp Oil (PCR) which is naturally rich in Cannabidiol (CBD), and has Cannabigerol (CBG), Cannabinol (CBN) Cannabichromene (CBC), terpenes, flavonoids and essential amino acids making it the ultimate broad spectrum oil. This oil works with our body's own endocannabinoid system (did you know you had one?), and so it interacts with all major systems in the physical body.

Considering my history and my personal stake in the products, I knew it had to be pure and consistent. Before we release any batch, our oils go through rigorous on-site and third-party lab testing. We provide these lab reports for every product on our website. I am so grateful to have CBD in my own life and love hearing of our customers experiences with them.

Now a happy, healthy human being, I love helping toxically overloaded people and their pets return to a more normal life! Also, through AlphaZelle, I help parents prevent their babies and children from becoming chemically sensitive and assist young people to retain their youthful appearance as they grow older.

I truly love this journey of healthy, vibrant living as we continue to expand our company. Now totally chemical free from A to Z with CBD, I know my good health starts with AlphaZelle!

**ABOUT THE AUTHOR:** Dale is an entrepreneur, product developer, and life-long student of wellness. Dale's inquisitive nature and her physical health issues led her to join numerous wellness companies from 1993-2003. Her passion was ignited when she discovered many of the products she used contained toxic ingredients that caused chemical sensitivity. This infused her mission to educate consumers about how to find safer products and replace toxic ones with healthy, eco-friendly versions. She founded AlphaZelle to offer healthy, eco-friendly, toxin-free household products for the whole family, including pets. Her Nature's Golden Miracle brand of CBD rounds out her product line providing a trustworthy, natural source for vitality and empowered living.

Dale F. Schock
AlphaZelle LLC
AlphaZelle.com
NGM-oil.com
dale@alphazelle.com ~ 973-288-1971

# Still I Rise, In God I Trust

*A Phenomenal Woman*

Melissa Lynn Dudley

I was always connected to God, though at times my faith wavered. I always had a deep sense of knowing, keen feeling, and innate wisdom on situations and events—sometimes even predicting events before they occurred. However, my authenticity and perfect identity were often suppressed by family and society. I was socially awkward and found it challenging to connect with people. I held deep compassion and unconditional love in my heart and could not reconcile how others did not share the same principles and instead often reacted with cruelty. Listening to my inution and wisdom got me through life; however, I was prideful of this and my pride got me into trouble. I wanted only to be perfectly myself and love and be loved unconditionally, yet for years I often found myself in situations that reflected anything but love.

On May 13, 2017, I lay in ICU with multiple organ failures, system failures, extreme malnutrition, and saddle pulmonary embolism, and a fifty percent survival rate. That day, oxygen dissipated, and I started to die. To be honest, given my life experiences, I wanted to die. I wanted an end to the emotional turmoil and mental anguish, and the feeling of my heart breaking and bleeding. I was fatigued by life and angry with God. My faith in Him and His presence wavered.

My thoughts focused on my children. I knew my daughters would be fine, but my two sons made my heart ache. My older son still needed guidance in his life. My youngest son, just over a year old, I worried for immensely, as I knew he would be diagnosed Autistic. I had to be here to serve as his advocate and guide. In that moment

I asked whomever was greater than me to save my life. In return, I made a covenant to discover my perfect identity and stop making toxic life choices.

From my diaphragm I felt a power rise and I said "Help." The angels, my nurse and other hospital staff, came in and intubated me in a medically induced coma so my body could rest and heal. I was woken a week later after they inserted a chest tube to drain a necrotic lung.

While I physically didn't die; I was reborn. When I woke from the coma; I had a deep knowing that if I wasn't successful in my covenant I would not survive.

In this covenant with God, I had agreed to listen to His guidance through my inner knowing and become the Perfect Person He created. To do this, I would have to relearn how to be; the identity I'd always known would have to be stripped away.

I spent almost eighty days in the hospital. I was so weak, simple actions like brushing my teeth and hair fatigued me instantly. It took six weeks to stand and walk again. During my stay, I was largely alone, except for the nursing staff. These caring, compassionate angels made life bearable as I slowly came to terms with my circumstances and wondered whether I would ever have a life again.

In August 2017, still weak but ambulatory, I was sent home in a hospital bed and with a feeding tube. My younger daughter, just sixteen at the time, was the primary caregiver for my younger son. I had not been able to hold him since a surgery I'd had back in February.

I soon found I was not assimilating or absorbing food. Eating or using the feeding tube caused me excruciating abdominal pain and spasms. A combination of opioids, benzodiazepines, and muscle relaxers brought me comfort but put me in a zombie-like state. My doctors soon stopped my medication, claiming my symptoms were psychosomatic. Though there was some truth to this, they were not being mindful or compassionate about what I was experiencing. (In fact, in October 2018 the Mayo Clinic would diagnose me with a central nervous system disorder called Central Sensitization Syndrome. Essentially, my central nervous system is completely sensitized and what I experience physically and emotionally is amplified at max power.)

By September, the constant pain was unbearable, and I considered ending my life. Once again, my younger son's fate stopped me. God told me if I took my life, those left to care for him would not be "safe"; only I could assist him in living a normal, happy and healthy life. In a last-ditch effort to find out the reason for my illness and in hopes I would be put on TPN (Total Parenteral Nutrition), I got checked into the hospital. Once again, the doctors had no answers, and TPN was not an option because of my history of blood clots and sepsis. I decided then to go rogue and figure out my own medical mystery. I would get in touch with my innate body wisdom.

I used a phone app to track what I ate and my gastrointestinal responses, eliminating all but five core foods I could tolerate. I found inventive ways to create delectable dishes and engaged in the enjoyment of meal preparation to nourish my body with love. I slowly started stretching myself and my endurance, moving more each day. I also organized and reorganized my surroundings, decluttering both my physical space and mind.

By May 2018 my feeding tube had been removed and I moved to another city to begin the next leg of my healing journey. I had to regain my independence and begin raising my son. Achieving this meant I had to gain emotional maturity, mental clarity, and resolve emotional loss in my heart. I had to heal myself of all the identity distortion developed in my lifetime, all the way back to conception by resolving my C-PTSD, Borderline Personality Disorder, and psychosis.

This initiation began on July 17, 2018, with an incident involving my husband. It impacted my younger daughter, and I knew I could not let this type of event to keep occurring. I gave myself a year to free myself from this vicious cycle, another covenant I made with God. I had to rely on Him to guide me through this. He made it abundantly clear: if I sought help I would be institutionalized, and my son taken away. My resolve was to break through my current distorted reality and work through my mind dysmorphia to my perfect identity.

It was during this time that I truly found my courage, resilience, and strength. Most nights I passed out in exhaustion from blessing the floor with my tears and snot as my heart cried out in pain. I was alone, having been abandoned by everyone in my life, including the two who meant the most to me, my mother and husband.

God sent two young women into my life to guide me through this experience. One, a neighbor, showed me great love and a new way to communicate with others in a nonjudgmental way. The other, whom I met online, became my earth guide and angel. She also had a deep connection with God and assisted me in working through my mind dysmorphia and the turmoil of my heart; she also taught me to stand tall in my truth instead of reacting with self-defensive behaviors. She walked me to God. Neither of these women doubted my sanity; they understood I was working through years of trauma and identity distortion.

As I began to rely on my innate wisdom and intuition, or God, I was guided to start journaling. This not only assisted me in untangling my mind but helped me to set and achieve goals and give my sub-conscious instructions on things I wanted to work on within myself. I started using oracle cards to "see" into myself and determine what I had to release. I started giving readings to others, with impeccable accuracy. I learned I had been given a blessing of Prophetic Word and assisting people to find their own perfect identity, passion, purpose, and plan. I can relay what God desires them to know and work on within themselves.

I used self-care, honor, tantra, and masturbation to heal my womb and heart, find my self-love, and create the person I desired to be internally and externally. I conditioned my brainstem, the part of the brain which desires stability and safety, to see change as stable and safe. I moved into a constant state of transformation, ever-changing and evolving. I gave myself instructions on what aspects in myself needing changing and conditioned my brain to those changes which allowed me to shift my habits and behaviors.

This journey was not only about overcoming trauma at the hands of others, but due to my own sinful choices. I had to admit them, and I had to forgive myself. Most difficult was admitting to my husband that I had tricked him into getting me pregnant with our son. An Angel had told me I would have a son and even let me know when it was time to get pregnant; however, instead of speaking to my then significant other regarding our child and allowing God to orchestrate the pregnancy, I got on birth control but did not take it.

Control had always been my way to survive; now, in order to shift my circumstances, I learned to be still, live my life in the present moment and experience. The lesson learned was to release control of all outcomes and allow God. God has shown me through focusing on my present moment, experience, and environment, and allowing Him to handle everything else, I am in infinite supply of all I need to lead a life of love, peace and joy. The only thing required of me is to focus on my passion, purpose, and plan and be a wonderful mother to my children.

I was also able to end my suicidal tendencies, with which I had struggled throughout my life. As a teenager, my identity was severely suppressed, leaving me in despair and feeling like I didn't belong on this planet. I attempted suicide multiple times and had several hospital admissions. I also considered ending my life three times during my awakening, the third time after another incident with my husband. The next day I packed my child up and embarked on a six-hour trip to deliver him to my husband before making my grand exit. While in the car, I got a message from my great-grandmother. She literally took over my body and drove for me, during which time I was completely unaware of my surroundings. Three hours into the drive I stopped for gas and my Earth Angel and close friend called me. Somehow, I got back on the highway heading toward my home. When I fully "returned" to my body and realized I was close to my exit, I accepted it as a sign that I was not to end my life but to continue finding my courage and resilience. I left suicidal behaviors behind for good that day.

Through this process I learned mindful and intuitive living, experiencing life in the present moment and embodying the habits and behaviors of a virtuous person. I have gone through three phases with God, the first of which was a baptism by fire—my NDE and my commitment to become His Child and discover my perfect identity. The second was a baptism by immersion, when I accepted Jesus Christ as my savior and washed my sins away. The third phase began when I made a full devotion of heart, soul, and power to God during my anointing by the Holy Spirit on December 10 and 11, 2019.

I am not nearly done growing into God's Child. I am entering 2020 a different person from the one who entered 2019. I will not be the same person entering into 2021 that I am today. I have full belief and faith that through this process I will fully embody Jesus Christ in my heart, mind, and soul, just as I know God is answering my prayer in showing me how to live a life of peace, love, and joy.

**ABOUT THE AUTHOR:** Melissa Lynn Dudley holds a bachelor's degree in business and spent ten years in corporate Financial Planning and Analysis (FP&A). Complications from a surgery in 2017 resulted in a serious central nervous system condition; it also became a catalyst for a complete spiritual, mental, and physical overhaul. Melissa experienced a healing with God and is currently working toward her health coach certification with a vision of inspiring and empowering others to find their perfect identity through charitable acts and community engagement. A proud mother of four, Melissa resides in Tampa, Florida with her two sons; her two adult daughters live Panama City, Florida.

Melissa Lynn Dudley
The Lotus, The Rose, The Yoni & Passion
face-book.com/TheLotusTheRoseTheYoniandPassion
thecompassionatenarcissist@gmail.com
720-557-7904

# Woke, Aware & Empowered
## LeNae Goolsby, JD

*"We are not human beings having a spiritual experience; we are spiritual beings having a human experience." ~ Pierre Teilhard de Chardin*

If you ever want to find out how really "enlightened" you are, spend the holidays at a theme park. I am writing this (in part) from the Cabana Bay Resort in Orlando, Florida during the Christmas-to-New Year school and work break. For the holidays this year, like two years prior, my husband and I decided to bring our two sons for a few days to Universal Studios, as well as a couple of days at selected Disney parks. For the most part the experience has been enjoyable, but not without its hiccups, and truth be told, more than once, I allowed myself to be pulled into the reactionary behavior of the 3D mass mind. So, I have room for improvement…always. But let me tell you a bit about how far I've come…

I will never forget one particular evening when I was sitting on my sofa after surviving another depressing day at the office. With Riedel wine glass in hand, emptying out the last of the Chardonnay, I was watching a mindless evening soap opera called "Revenge." I was also plotting a little revenge of my own.

See, in that moment I had a list of a few people and an entire organization that I really wanted to take down. I wanted to transfer my pain to every single one of them, because they were to blame, or so I thought, for my wretched situation. Then, like a V8 smack to the head (Do you remember those commercials? *"I could have had a V8!"*), I suddenly realized that I was attempting to numb my pain with wine and get revenge lessons from one of the dumbest shows on television. All of a sudden I realized that the path I was on was only going to take me deeper and deeper into a state of being that compromised any hope of ever being back on top, and quite frankly was a great plan to land in jail. Things were dark, yes, but at least I wasn't in prison. There was still much I could lose if I didn't snap out of it.

I realize I'm being vague about what those people and that organization did to land me in such a destructive state...suffice it to say my husband and I found ourselves six figures in debt and I was buying into the role of the victim. The expanded version of this story is in my book, "*Seven Sundays to Sweet Inner Serenity—how to cultivate the calm even in the midst of the crazy chaos.*" What I'm talking about here is what has happened since.

About seven years have passed, and both the show and my vengeful imaginings have long been cancelled. But make no mistake about it, while the choice to forgo "lighting a match" to the lives of those I blamed at the time was immediate, by no means did I all of a sudden become woke, aware, and empowered. That took years, and in fact is still in a state of evolution.

Shortly after the Universe smacked me in the head, I heard Wayne Dyer talk about the quote with which I begin this chapter. While I'd heard this concept—namely that we are primarily spiritual beings wearing skin suits for the purposes of learning and growing on this physical plane—it had never truly broken through the dogma of my Protestant upbringing. However, in that singular moment, the stressors in my human life experience suddenly seemed very temporal, very insignificant, even. That said, because of my "fundamental Christian" raising, I had a lot of questions I needed answered, and even more beliefs that were not really mine to shed.

For example, I became somewhat obsessed with understanding what really happens when we die because what I had been taught in church was (a) based on men's interpretation of what was written in the Bible, (b) was being proselytized by men who had never actually died, and (c) involved a lot of rules and fear. About that time, both

Dr. Eben Alexander and Anita Moorjani both came out with books discussing their personal Near-Death Experiences (NDEs). I also read Annie Kagan's *The Afterlife of Billy Fingers: How my bad boy brother proved to me there's life after death,* in which she channels her brother as he speaks of his death experience. Also, I discovered Kelli Coffee of "Kelli in the Raw" on YouTube, who talked about her NDE.

While each person had a unique afterlife experience, they were all comparable, and none of them sounded remotely like anything I was taught in church. In fact, each one, whether or not they were "saved" in the Christian sense of the word, only experienced love, and all came to understand their role as the Creator of their experience. Accepting myself as the Creator of my life experience took a lot of reconditioning. After all, I had been raised to believe that I needed "saving" lest I burn for all eternity in hell.

These were still other people's experiences, and I certainly was not interested in playing a game of "Flatliners" myself, so how to discern Truth? Enter "Applied Kinesiology."

Applied Kinesiology (AK), according to Wikipedia, is "a technique in alternative medicine claimed to be able to diagnose illness or choose treatment by testing muscles for strength and weakness." Alternately, and possibly more correctly, the process can be used as a truth detector, a source of guidance that connects us to infinite wisdom or the field of pure potentiality as well. In the most basic of layman's terms, our muscles are directly linked to our nervous system and our nervous system is our electrical network. When pressure is applied to our muscles, if the information is "false" the muscles go weak, but if the information is "true" then the muscles will hold their strength. There is a superior explanation to this in *Power versus Force* by Dr. David A. Hawkins, and there are many videos on its application on YouTube.

When I was first introduced to AK I was so excited because I'd finally found a practical technique that I could implement to help me discern how people are actually showing up (in other words, whether or not they could be trusted). This has always been particularly challenging for me because I often see people's potential—potential they themselves cannot see and quite frankly may never realize. While in theory this sounds wonderful, from a business perspective, particularly from a hiring perspective, it is not that great. I subsequently began to "muscle test" to determine whether or not an applicant for a position at Infinite Health IMC would be a qualified and profitable fit.

Shortly thereafter I moved from physical "muscle testing" to the use of a pendulum to ascertain truth. The pendulum operates on the same principles as AK; for me, however, it was a particularly helpful tool because it provided clear *visual* answers. This was important because at the time, I was still second-guessing my decisions about people, business…about nearly every single choice I made up to that point—from hiring people, to trusting vendors, to which bills I could safely pay.

Eventually, I became less dependent on the pendulum and became more reliant on my own intuition. Now the process of hiring is easier because I trust myself, and the level of individual our business is attracting. I no longer second-guess myself the way I used to…at all. Do I still use a muscle test or use the pendulum? Yes, every once in a while for validation. I will also get validation from my husband who has become quite adept at ascertaining positive versus negative answers to questions simply by "tuning in" to feelings in his body. He closes his eyes and poses the yes or no question and then either feels an expansion in his chest (this means yes), or a constriction in his gut (this means no).

I also use AK to make fun decisions. For example, if at a new restaurant, which item on the menu will I enjoy the most? Or, if I go to this event, will I actually have fun? I even used AK to help me narrow down a pile of books I'd picked out to purchase at Barnes and Noble one time. I have friends who employ this method to ensure that their food and supplement choices are on point to nourish their bodies. If there is a question to be asked AK is a great tool to harness, at least until one is fully confident their ability to access their intuitive knowing without second-guessing themselves.

For years I was a seeker devouring information that challenged, and in some cases even refuted, what I was conditioned to believe. I've learned that we actually live in a sort of backwards reality where what we've been led to believe by various institutions (educational, religious, government, etc.) about the world, about the Universe, and about ourselves is the opposite of how things really are; for example, a world of matter versus a world of constantly moving microparticles that give the appearance of solid matter...and a world where the observer has no effect on outcome, versus a world where the observer absolutely affects the outcome of a thing (ergo the power of thoughts, feelings, beliefs, and prayer).

Having gained new insights, new understandings, expanding my awareness and consciousness, knowing now that I am the Creator of my experience, that there is no God separate and apart from me, and that what I experience external to me is a reflection of my inner being has been paramount to moving out of a victim, dis-empowered mindset to an empowered state of being. For the most part I no longer allow the influences of others (including family members, friends, societal opinions, etc.) to dictate to me who I am, what I think, or how I feel.

Make no mistake about it, accepting one's self as the Creator of her/his life is not rainbows and butterflies. It is so easy to buy into the delusion that we are the victims of our circumstances, that our situation is not our fault.

For example, in 2012 when I was living in Lake Charles, Louisiana (a town I loathed because at the time I perceived it to be filled with small-minded, petty, and gossiping people), my husband and I were six-figures in business debt, I had no local friends because I was not a local and did not go to the "right" high-school (because high school attendance is how you are judged in Lake Charles), nor did I have any hope or clue as to how to fix a dern thing, it was easy to blame "God" for allowing me to be there, blame my husband for moving us there, blame all the low-level dredges of that town for putting me in that situation. Coming to the realization that I'd actually created my situation, and that it all was happening FOR me, as opposed to happening TO me, was a significantly more difficult pill to swallow. It was also a significantly more empowering pill to swallow.

Coming in to the realization that I create the good and I create the less than desirable in my life, empowered me to see it all as information…information designed to guide me to create a more aware, awake, and empowered life experience.

This is not, however, to be confused with a "perfect" life experience. Being "woke" is not at all about being perfect, or even about being spiritually "superior" (a comical idea to say the least). *"… We are spiritual beings having a human experience;"* accordingly, a large part of having this human experience is embracing all that the human experience provides…including being mindful of who I am while in a ninety-minute theme park line surrounded by a sleeping mass of people all waiting for a two-minute roller coaster ride.

**ABOUT THE AUTHOR:** LeNae Goolsby, JD is the Co-Founder of Infinite Health Integrative Medicine Center in Louisiana, an elite precision medicine practice with a niche focus on health optimization, longevity, and regenerative medicines. Additionally, LeNae is a best-selling author, empowerment-centric speaker, and consultant. LeNae is the co-author of *Empower Your Life* and *Empowered Medicine: Harnessing the Laws of the Universe for Optimized Health,* and the author of *Seven Sundays to Sweet Inner Serenity: How to cultivate the calm even in the midst of the chaos*, as well as other empowerment-centric e-books available on Amazon.com.

LeNae Goolsby, JD
Infinite Health Integrative Medicine Center
YourInfiniteHealth.com
LeNaeGoolsby.com
LeNae.Goolsby@gmail.com

# About the Authors

**Are you inspired by the stories in this book?
Let the authors know.**

**See the contact information at the end of each chapter
and reach out to them.**

**They'd love to hear from you!**

*Author Rights & Disclaimer*

*Each author in this book retains the copyright and all inherent rights to their individual chapter. Their stories are printed herein with each author's permission.*

*Each author is responsible for the individual opinions expressed through their words. Powerful You! Publishing bears no responsibility for the content of the stories by these authors.*

# Acknowledgements & Gratitude

OUR HEARTS ARE FILLED WITH GRATITUDE for the many wonderful individuals who have come together with such open hearts to lift and awaken the world to a more conscious state of joy, love, possibility, and empowerment.

To the authors of these stories we applaud you, honor you, and love you. You exemplify resilience, courage, selflessness and, even more than these, you radiate pure love and the beauty of the human spirit. We are honored to share this journey with you, and so grateful that you stepped fully into your power by offering your own story to light the way for others. You are a beautiful example of love in action.

There are many beautiful souls who we gratefully call our tribe who offer their guidance, expertise, love, and support!

Our editor Dana Micheli who knows the deep questions to ask to get to the heart and essence of the stories. We are so very grateful for you.

Our awesome training team, AmondaRose Igoe, Kathy Sipple, and Karen Flaherty—your caring hearts and vast expertise light the way for our authors. We love and appreciate each of you!

Ruth Kent, enlightened spirit and wayshower – Your words are a masterpiece of inspired truth to light the way for our authors to shine.

Our friends and families, we love you! Your unwavering, loving support of our inspirations and projects continue to allow us to faithfully pursue our passion and vision for life.

Above all, we are grateful for the Divine Spirit that flows through us each day providing continued blessings, lessons, and opportunities for growth, peace and JOY!

Namaste` and Blessings, Love, and Gratitude,
Sue Urda and Kathy Fyler

# About Sue Urda and Kathy Fyler

Sue and Kathy have been friends for 30 years and business partners since 1994. They have received many awards and accolades for their businesses over the years and continue to love the work they do and the people they do it with. As publishers, they are honored to help people share their stories, passions, and lessons.

Their mission is to raise the vibration of people and the planet and to connect and empower women in their lives. Their calling has been years in the making and is a gift from Spirit.

The strength of their partnership lies in their deep respect, love, and understanding of one another as well as their complementary skills and knowledge. Kathy is a technology enthusiast, web goddess, and free-thinker. Sue is an author and speaker with a love of creative undertakings. Their honor, love, and admiration for each other are boundless.

Together their energies combine to feed the flames of countless women who are seeking truth, empowerment, joy, peace, and connection with themselves, their own spirits, and other women.

Connect with Sue and Kathy:

Powerful You! Inc.
239-280-0111
info@powerfulyou.com
PowerfulYouPublishing.com
SueUrda.com

# About Ruth M. Kent

I am a mother and retired Intensive care/trauma - Registered Nurse, a Certified Emotion Code and Body Code Practitioner, the Creator of "The Success Together Program". My Faith is my source from which I draw my fearlessness in my service and leadership. I am an inspired writer, speaker and creator, and a sought-after mentor and healer. Known for my authenticity, "I walk my talk" as an enlightened intuitive in all areas of life and it is a gift that I share with the world. I am humbled by the trust and value gifted to me for my unlimited unconditional love. My willingness is my wisdom.

Today, my work as a certified Emotion Code and Body Code practitioner and mentor is dedicated to helping people discover joy and abundance by getting to the core cause. Since 2007, I've been blessed to share this work with the world, witnessing countless miracles in my client's lives. I work with clients one-on-one and in small groups using the Body Code and the Emotion Code systems to allow individuals to step into and live life from the greatest version of themselves and go beyond symptoms to unlock their highest potential.

Connect with Ruth:

Website: ruthkentllc.com
Facebook: facebook.com/ruthkentllc
LinkedIn: linkedin.com/in/ruth-m-kent-37768132
Instagram: instagram.com/ruthkentllc
Email: ruthkentpresent@gmail.com

# Are You Called to be an Author?

If you're like most people, you may find the prospect of writing a book daunting. Where to begin? How to proceed? No worries! We're here to help.

Whether you choose to contribute to an anthology or write your own book using our QuickPublish Formula™, we'll be your guiding light, professional consultant, and enthusiastic supporter. If you can see yourself as an author partnering with a publishing company who has your best interest at heart and with the expertise to back it up, we'd be honored to be your publisher.

We provide personalized guidance through the writing and editing process. We offer complete publishing packages and our service is designed for a personal and optimal authoring experience.

We are committed to helping individuals express their voice and shine their light into the world. Are you ready to start your journey as an author? Do it with Powerful You! Publishing.

Powerful You! Publishing
239-280-0111
powerfulyoupublishing.com

# Anthology Books

Empowering Transformations for Women
Women Living Consciously
Journey to Joy
Pathways to Vibrant Health & Well-Being
Women Living Consciously Book II
Healthy, Abundant, and Wise
Keys to Conscious Business Growth
The Gifts of Grace & Gratitude
Heal Thy Self
Empower Your Life
Heart & Soul
The Beauty of Authenticity

## Other Books

Powerful Intentions, Everyday Gratitude - Books I & II
Let Me Walk the Journey with You
Medicine Jewelry – Working with Rock People
Led By Purpose
Divinely Fit
A Journey Back to Restoration
Seven Sundays to Sweet Inner Serenity
Live Beyond Your Loss
Frankie: My Brother, My Hero
The Power of Love and Awakening Consciousness

# Allow
# Your
# Awakening